U.S. Department of Justice
Office of Justice Programs
National Institute of Justice

I0448812

NIJ

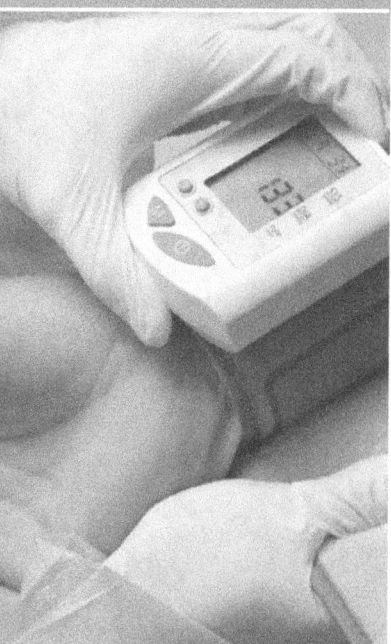

Corrections Today . . . and Tomorrow:
A Compilation of Corrections-Related Articles

www.ojp.usdoj.gov/nij

U.S. Department of Justice
Office of Justice Programs
810 Seventh Street N.W.
Washington, DC 20531

Michael B. Mukasey
Attorney General

Jeffrey L. Sedgwick
Acting Assistant Attorney General

David W. Hagy
Director, National Institute of Justice

This and other publications and products of the National Institute
of Justice can be found at:

National Institute of Justice
www.ojp.usdoj.gov/nij

Office of Justice Programs
Innovation • Partnerships • Safer Neighborhoods
www.ojp.usdoj.gov

Contents

NIJ's Response to the Prison Rape Elimination Act

By National Institute of Justice Staff

Authors' note: Points of view expressed in this article do not represent the official position or policies of the U.S. Department of Justice.

Sexual assault in the nation's prisons continues to be a complex problem of concern to both prison officials and policy-makers. To date, few research studies have investigated sexual violence in specific correctional institutions, and their results cannot be extrapolated to the national prison population due to how limited the studies were.

Understanding the need to determine the magnitude, culture and repercussions of sexual violence in prisons nationwide, Congress passed and President Bush signed into law the Prison Rape Elimination Act (PREA) of 2003. The act sets a zero tolerance for rape and sexual assault in prisons and calls for:

- Developing and instituting national standards to prevent, detect and reduce sexual violence in prisons;
- Making data and information on sexual violence more available to correctional administrators; and
- Making prisons more accountable for inmate safety.

In response to PREA, the National Institute of Justice, the research, development and evaluation arm of the U.S. Department of Justice, has undertaken a number of studies and related activities to provide more information on prison rape, including its relationship to prison culture; the effectiveness of sexual victimization prevention programs; and ways to assess the risk of sexual violence. NIJ will also be studying how perpetrators are investigated and prosecuted and the impact of sexual violence on victims. Once collected, this information will be used to help improve how correctional facilities address sexual violence among inmates.

A National Study

Soon after PREA became law, NIJ awarded a grant to Mark Fleisher, Ph.D., of Case Western University to conduct one of the first national research projects on prison rape — an anthropological study of inmate culture in medium- and maximum-security prisons for men and women across the United States. No other research has studied prison rape in terms of inmate culture and the social and sexual climate found in prisons.

Instead of gathering data from prison records, the researchers are conducting anonymous and confidential interviews with inmates to understand their perspective on consensual and coercive sex and rape. The study's goal is to clearly define what constitutes sexual activity in prisons and to help both policy-makers and practitioners better understand the differences between consensual, coercive and predatory sex in prisons. Names and locations of the inmates and participating prison facilities will not be released.

One of the challenges of Fleisher's research is that inmates do not normally use terms like "consensual sex" and "coercive sex," and their descriptions of these acts are often ambiguous because their social and sexual interactions are intertwined.

When the research is completed, nearly 400 male inmates and 200 female inmates will have been interviewed. In the preliminary findings, researchers found that as the number of inmates interviewed grew, themes and similarities started emerging. For example, most inmates described a likely target of prison rape in exactly the same way: young, small, white, with feminine physical features and body movements. Inmates also described the typical victim as a person with no prison experience, friends, companions or social support. However, they also agreed that inmates' fear of prison rape is low.

The main source of inmates' knowledge of prison sex appears to come from their conversations with other inmates. Inmates usually do not report information about prison sex that they personally experienced or observed. They report what they have seen or heard from other inmates, friends who were inmates or the movies. They then blend these accounts with their own prison experiences so that they sound as if they actually witnessed numerous acts of rape.

Research Solicitations

In addition to Fleisher's study, NIJ has solicited research on the following topics:

Prevention — Identifying and evaluating sexual victimization prevention programs in correctional institutions;

Risk assessment — Creating and validating instruments that assess the risk of sexual violence for victims and predators; and

Medical-psychological impact — Assessing the medical and psychological impact that being a victim of sexual violence has on inmates.

To date, NIJ has awarded four research grants in these topic areas: Two on prevention programs and two on risk assessment.

Prevention. In one of the projects to identify effective prevention programs, researchers at the Urban Institute in Washington, D.C., are determining what sexual victimization programs exist in men's and women's prisons. In the other project, investigators from the Colorado Division of Criminal Justice are identifying prevention programs that exist in jails and juvenile facilities. In both projects, scientists are using objective measures that include performance measures and evidence-based practices to identify successful programs. They will detail case studies and describe model programs that prison administrators could adopt or modify to improve their own facilities.

Risk Assessment. Two risk-assessment projects will develop techniques to better help correctional officers identify sexual predators and potential victims among incoming inmates. In one project,

the James F. Austin Institute will rely on official reports of sexual violence generated during the past three years by a state that thoroughly investigates all allegations of rape in its prison system. These reports will be used to develop a profile of inmates most likely to become victims or predators. Environmental factors and facility design will also be considered in constructing the risk-assessment instrument. In the other project, researchers at the University of Virginia will design a risk-assessment tool to help identify potential victims and predators of sexual violence in prisons. This project will examine the traits of inmates who were victims or predators and the correctional environment where the assaults took place.

Medical-Psychological Impact. NIJ is reviewing research proposals on the medical and psychological impact of sexual violence on inmates in correctional facilities, how it affects their ability to reenter society, and how correctional departments and their partners investigate and prosecute allegations of sexual violence. NIJ expects to request research proposals on the characteristics of sexual violence as it pertains to violent behavior in correctional facilities overall.

Protecting Human Research Subjects

Research on prison sexual violence is very sensitive, especially if it includes interviews of inmates. Under PREA, research could involve reviewing any number of confidential records, including incident reports and medical records, which could invade an individual's privacy if not conducted with sensitivity and under top security.

Protecting the privacy and rights of human research subjects, including prison inmates, is of the utmost importance. To address this issue, NIJ is conducting a series of meetings on the protection of human research subjects. Experts on corrections research, human subjects policies and sexual violence in prison are meeting to develop a set of protocols to help researchers and institutional review boards understand and comply with the human rights protection policies necessary to conduct effective research in a prison setting.

A Research Review

To date, researchers have used varying approaches, methodologies and definitions to describe prison sexual violence research, which has resulted in wide-ranging rates for the incidence and prevalence of prison rape. To encapsulate this information, NIJ staff have written a comprehensive review of the published research titled *Prison Rape: A Critical Review of the Literature* (for more information, see references). The review describes the research on prison sexual violence since 1968 and analyzes the challenges and problems that must be overcome to effectively measure sexual assault in correctional institutions. The review discusses problems and issues that

develop when comparing facilities and makes suggestions for future research.

A Look to the Future

Sexual assault and violence perpetrated on inmates in correctional facilities has many social, physical, psychological and economic costs and repercussions, both inside and outside of prisons. PREA may help to sharply reduce these and many other consequences of institutional sexual violence by making prison rape prevention a higher priority in federal, state and local prison systems. The results of the research and related activities that NIJ is funding will help develop and carry out national standards to detect, prevent and reduce prison rape and sexual violence and punish the perpetrators.

REFERENCES

Data Collection for the Prison Rape Elimination Act of 2003. 2004. Washington, D.C.: Bureau of Justice Statistics. Available at www.ojp.usdoj.gov/bjs/pub/pdf/dcprea 03.pdf.

Gaes, G.G., and A.L. Goldberg. 2004. *Prison Rape: A Critical Review of the Literature*, executive summary and working paper. Available at www.nicic.org/Library/019813.

NIJ Annual Report to Congress. 2005. Washington, D.C.: National Institute of Justice.

Annual Report to Congress in response to the Prison Rape Elimination Act. 2004. Public Law 108-79, National Institute of Corrections. ◆

Reprinted with permission of the American Correctional Association, Lanham, MD, February 2006.

Brief Mental Health Screening For Corrections Intake

By Andrew L. Goldberg and Brian R. Higgins

Authors' note: Points of view expressed in this article do not represent the official position or policies of the U.S. Department of Justice.

Correctional administrators need brief, cost-effective, easy-to-administer and reliable mental health screens to initially identify mentally ill detainees, who can become disruptive and a threat to themselves and others. Current mental health screening at corrections intake varies greatly — from one or two questions to a full-scale clinical analysis. Available instruments are often costly and time-consuming, making them impractical for daily screening of a large number of inmates at intake. As a result, even though most prisons and jails screen inmates for mental illness during booking,[1] research has shown that they miss the majority of inmates with mental health problems, particularly those with less obvious symptoms.[2]

Researchers, through funding by the National Institute of Justice (NIJ), have now developed and validated two brief, free mental health screening tools that proved effective in identifying various levels of mentally ill detainees at intake: the Correctional Mental Health Screen (CMHS)[3] and the Brief Jail Mental Health Screen (BJMHS).[4] The screens use standard one-page questionnaires that correctional officers with modest training can administer in three to five minutes and score simply by adding up "yes" answers.

Both screens proved valid when compared with far longer and more detailed screens administered by trained clinical assessors. The CMHS screens were effective in identifying nine categories of mental disorder in both male and female inmates. The BJMHS was effective in identifying male inmates with mental disorders and is being refined to increase its effectiveness in identifying female detainees with anxiety- and stress-related mental illness.

Using the Screening Instruments

CMHS. The CMHS uses separate questionnaires for men and women: the Correctional Mental Health Screen–Male (CMHS–M) asks 12 yes/no questions, and the Correctional Mental Health Screen–Female (CMHS–F) asks eight yes/no questions about current and lifetime indications of serious mental disorder. Both screens take about three to five minutes to administer. Six questions regarding symptoms and history of mental illness appear on both questionnaires, including whether the inmate ever has been hospitalized for nonmedical, including psychiatric, reasons. The remaining questions on each test focus on types of mental disorders more prevalent in that gender. It is recommended that male inmates who answer five or more questions "yes" and female inmates who answer four or more questions "yes" be referred for further evaluation.

BJMHS. The BJMHS is an eight-item yes/no questionnaire that takes about two to three minutes and requires minimal training to administer; it asks six questions about current mental disorders and two about any history of hospitalization or medication for mental or emotional problems. Inmates who answer "yes" to two or more questions about current mental disorders or acknowledge having been hospitalized or taking medication for mental or emotional problems are referred for further evaluation. Instructions for administering the screen appear on the back of the form. Correctional classification officers, intake staff or nursing staff can administer the screen without specialized mental health training, but may receive brief informal training before administration.

The Correctional Mental Health Screen

First phase. The researchers combined into one composite interview questions from five screening modules for a range of mental disorders.[5] The resulting Composite Mental Health Screen consisted of 53 items and took about 25 minutes to administer.

Researchers then administered the composite screen to randomly selected adult detainees in Connecticut's five jails (four for men and one for women) within 24 to 76 hours after admission. Inmates younger than 18, those considered high-risk or in restricted housing, and those already under medical or mental health care were excluded. Twenty percent of those screened underwent a comprehensive (45-minute to three-hour) clinical assessment using a combination of instruments. The results of the composite screen were compared with the clinical assessments and information about the inmates from correctional records, including mental health scores and overall risk scores.

Second phase. After comparing the test results, the researchers eliminated the questions with the fewest variations in answers. They then separately analyzed two samples, each consisting of one-half of the composite screen interviews. They used the results of these analyses to determine which questions best predicted nine diagnoses of mental illness associated with emotional and behavioral instability (including risk of harm to

self or others). Problems adhering to the facility's activity schedule and disciplinary standards were also considered.

Based on their analyses, the researchers selected 12 questions for male inmates and eight questions for female inmates, which they tested on 206 inmates. Follow-up clinical assessments showed that the screens identified both male and female inmates with serious mental disorders in all nine categories. The screens proved highly valid in identifying depression, anxiety, full and partial posttraumatic stress disorders (PTSD), selected personality disorders, and the presence of any current mental disorder. Using a cutoff score of five or more "yes" answers, the CHMS–M was 75.5 percent accurate in identifying male inmates with a previously undetected mental illness. Using a cutoff score of four or more "yes" answers, the CHMS–F was 75 percent accurate in identifying female inmates with a previously undetected mental illness.

The clinical assessments found the incidence of serious mental illness among the inmates to be far higher than in the general population and comparable to that in psychiatric settings. This finding is especially significant given that inmates who had already been referred for mental health care because of obvious behavioral signs of mental illness or a history of mental health hospitalization were excluded from the screening.

Recommendations. Based on interviews with officers who administered the screens, the researchers suggest the following improvements for the administration procedure:

- Provide additional informal training to clarify the purpose of the screen and improve interviewing and probing techniques;
- Have nurses, if available, administer the tool to uncooperative inmates or those who feel uncomfortable answering questions about symptoms of mental illness; and
- Offer a computer-assisted version of the tool, which may increase responses to questions.

The Brief Jail Mental Health Screen

The BJMHS is adapted from the Referral Decision Scale, a 14-item questionnaire designed to identify inmates with schizophrenia, bipolar disorder and serious depression. Although the Referral Decision Scale is effective in identifying inmates with mental illness, it is less so in diagnosing specific disorders and questions about lifetime rather than current symptoms may overestimate the need for current mental health treatment.[6]

Development/administration. The developers of the BJMHS shortened the Referral Decision Scale to eight questions and revised several questions to ask about current symptoms. Informally trained jail intake staff administered the screen during booking to both male and female detainees in four county jails, two in New York and two in Maryland, from May 2002 to January 2003. Nurses administered the screen to some inmates as part of a health screen or to inmates who were too intoxicated to answer the questions during booking. Twelve percent of the inmates screened using the BJMHS were referred for further assessment.

Validation. To validate the BJMHS, trained clinical assessors administered the Structured Clinical Interview for DSM–IV, a longer and more detailed instrument that identifies lifetime and current mental disorders, on a sample of inmates who had undergone screening. The sample included both male and female inmates, and inmates who had and had not been referred for assessment on the basis of the BJMHS. They found that the BJMHS correctly classified 74 percent of male inmates and 62 percent of female inmates.

However, 35 percent of the female inmates who were not identified for referral by the BJMHS were diagnosed as mentally ill based on the clinical interview. The researchers discovered that the instrument did not measure symptoms of anxiety associated with the high incidence of PTSD among female detainees. NIJ is currently funding additional research through spring of 2007 to examine these cases and adapt the BJMHS to include questions that would measure these conditions.

Conclusion

The CMHS, because it uses separate questionnaires for men and women, proved effective in identifying both male and female inmates in need of mental health treatment. Also, excluding obviously mentally ill inmates from the screen highlighted its ability to identify those inmates whose symptoms were less obvious. The high rates of mental disorder found in the follow-up clinical assessment indicate the screen's potential utility in helping provide the correct diagnosis and treatment for those inmates. The BJMHS proved effective in screening male inmates but was less effective for female inmates. Thus, the instrument is being refined by adding items related to stress and anxiety disorders that are more prevalent among female inmates.

Both screens hold promise as powerful tools for standardizing and increasing the accuracy of initial mental health screening in correctional facilities. Their effectiveness in identifying inmates in need of mental health treatment compares favorably with the longer, more cumbersome, and training-intensive tools used in the clinical assessments. Their brevity, use of yes/no questions, simple scoring techniques and availability at no cost make them well-suited for quick mental health screening of large numbers of inmates during booking.

For copies of the instruments and the full grant reports, visit www.ncjrs.org/pdffiles1/nij/grants/210829.pdf andwww.ncjrs.org/pdffiles1/nij/grants/213805.pdf.

ENDNOTES

[1]Beck, A. and L. Maruschak. 2001. *Mental health treatment in state prisons, 2000.* Special Report. Washington, DC: U.S. Department of Justice, Bureau of Justice Statistics. Available at http://www.ojp.usdoj.gov/bjs/abstract/mhtsp00.htm.

Steadman, H. and B. Veysey. 1997. *Providing services for jail inmates with mental disorder.* Research in Brief. Washington, DC: U.S. Department of Justice, National Institute of Justice. Available at http://www.ncjrs.gov/pdffiles/162207.pdf.

[2]Parsons, S., L. Walker and D. Grubin. 2001. Prevalence of mental disorder in female remand prisons. *Journal of Forensic Psychiatry.* 12(1):194–202.

Teplin, L. 1990. Detecting disorder: The treatment of mental illness among jail detainees. *Journal of Consulting and Clinical Psychology*, 58(2):233–236.

[3]Ford, J. and R. Trestman. 2005. *Evidence-based enhancement of the detection, prevention, and treatment of mental illness in correctional systems*, Final report. Available at www.ncjrs.org/pdffiles1/nij/grants/210829.pdf.

[4]Osher, F., J. Scott, H. Steadman and P. Robbins. 2004. *Validating a brief jail mental health screen*, Final technical report. Available at www.ncjrs.org/pdffiles1/nij/grants/213805.pdf. For more information on this study, see also: Steadman, H., J. Scott, F. Osher, T. Agnese and P. Robbins. 2005. Validation of the brief jail mental health screen. *Psychiatric Services*, 56(7): 816–822.

[5]The instruments used were the screening module for the Structured Clinical Interview for DSM–IV for major mental disorders; the Primary Care PTSD Screen for posttraumatic stress disorder; the Iowa Personality Disorder Screen; the Referral Decision Scale; and a substance use screen (not included in the final instruments).

[6]Veysey, B., H. Steadman, J. Morrissey, M. Johnson and J. Beckhead. 1998. Using the Referral Decision Scale to screen mentally ill detainees: Validity and implementation issues. *Law and Human Behavior*, 22(2): 305–315.

Andrew L. Goldberg, a social science analyst with the Office of Research and Evaluation at NIJ, monitors a number of programs including mental health for corrections. Brian R. Higgins is a senior writer/editor for Lockheed Martin Information Technology. Doris Wells, managing writer/editor for NIJ's update column in Corrections Today, *also contributed to this article.*

Helping Probation and Parole Officers Cope With Stress

By National Institute of Justice Staff

Author's Note: Opinions or points of view expressed in this article represent a consensus of the authors and do not represent the official position or policies of the U.S. Department of Justice.

Correctional agencies are losing money, losing good employees and jeopardizing officer and public safety due to work-related stress. An NIJ-funded study[1] to examine the causes and effects of stress on probation and parole officers found, surprisingly, that most of their work-related stress stems, not from physical dangers, but from high caseloads, overwhelming paperwork and excessive deadlines. The study also found that developing a stress reduction program can be an effective solution that can save money and enhance officer and public safety.

The Study

To identify the nature and scope of probation and parole officer stress, researchers reviewed published and unpublished materials on stress and related topics, selected nine stress-reduction programs for study, and talked with personnel at various levels of the American Probation and Parole Association. Researchers also conducted telephone interviews with individuals from five of the nine programs and conducted in-person interviews at the other four.

Physical dangers of the job. Probation and parole officer work can be dangerous. According to surveys performed in four states (New York, Pennsylvania, Texas and Virginia), between 39 percent and 55 percent of officers have been victims of work-related violence or threats.[2] The types and levels of stress vary with the nature of the work. For example, parole officers who work in a facility or community setting may be concerned for their own safety as well as the public's. Their work may have become even riskier because offenders on probation and parole commit more serious crimes than in the past, and more offenders have serious drug abuse histories and show less hesitation in using violence.[3] However, "danger on the job" was not cited as one of the three major sources of stress.

Three major sources of stress. Officers cited high case loads as the most common stress factor, followed by an overwhelming amount of paperwork and excessive deadlines.

- High caseloads: The average supervision caseload of a probation officer is very high — 139.
- Paperwork overload: Management information systems may help to reduce the load, but officers still face an enormous amount of paperwork.
- Deadline pressure: Too many unexpected or uncontrollable deadlines create undue stress and frustration.

Other causes. Many officers cited their supervisors as a source of stress. Researchers found that 87 percent of probation officers in one survey disliked their supervisors mainly because their supervisors did not recognize their achievements or appreciate their hard work.[4] Few advancement opportunities and low salaries were other reasons given. For example, the median salary for probation officers and correctional treatment specialists in 1999 was just over $36,000[5] and $39,000 in 2004.[6] Some officers cited low morale stemming from feelings of failure when blamed for offender misconduct and lack of public safety. Others said they got discouraged because they had limited options for imposing sanctions or offering rehabilitation to offenders.

How Do Officers Cope?

Probation and parole officers use a range of methods to relieve on-the-job stress.

Reactive methods. Some officers take extra sick leave — mental health days — simply to relieve the pressure. Others take sick leave to cope with stress-related health problems such as lower back pain or headaches. Some request transfers; others apply for early retirement.

Proactive methods. Most officers cited physical exercise as the most positive way to relieve stress. Others mentioned discussing cases with fellow officers, using religion, venting and talking to relatives.

Stress-Reduction Program

To address on-the-job stress, researchers recommend a stress-reduction program that can improve staff performance, enhance officer and public safety, and help save money. A stress-reduction program is designed to help prevent and relieve correctional officers' work-related stress. It can be structured in three basic forms:

- In-house programs, which consist of a separate unit within or operated by the correctional agency;
- External arrangements, which involve regular use of a private service provider; and
- Hybrid programs, which combine elements of both in-house and external structures.

The program can provide the following benefits:

- Reduce recruiting, screening and training costs associated with replacing employees, due to high turnover among probation and parole officers.
- Improve production by increasing morale and reducing backlogs or

stressful overload schedules of backup employees covering for co-workers on sick leave.

- Increase safety for staff and public by not being forced to delegate difficult and risky tasks of seasoned officers to rookies.

To create an effective stress-reduction program, agency administrators should consider the following when planning or expanding a program.

Select talented and dedicated staff with well-developed inter- personal skills. The quality of the staff is the backbone of the program. Administrators will need to decide whether to hire professional staff or train in-house staff. Outside professionals do not need training, but unlike in-house staff, they may not be very familiar with probation and parole issues.

Sell the program to administrators. Agency administrators must demonstrate concern for employee welfare and support the program. Involve middle managers and line supervisors who must grant permission for employee participation, which could count toward mandated training. Obtain the support of unions that could make or break a program at the management level.

Ensure confidentiality. Peer supporters and employees must establish the same confidentiality that exists between licensed mental health practitioners and clients.

Assess effectiveness. Evaluate a program to assess if it needs improvement. Evaluation should be built into program design and planning. In an outcome evaluation, the most compelling evidence is reduced stress.[7]

Provide adequate funding. Allow for one-time start-up costs. Minimize expenses by securing in-kind contributions and recruiting university professors as evaluators. Seek free resources and use any available experienced practitioners to help plan and evaluate.

Reduce organizational sources of stress. Individual agency managers should coordinate with the stress reduction program staff to identify and reduce any controllable agency-based sources of stress.

Outlook

When asked to describe his level of stress, one officer said: "Yes, I take mental health days. I use them, and I get in trouble a lot, but it's a case of self-preservation."[8] Agencies can use a stress reduction program to help this officer and others like him. Findings from this study indicate that such programs show great promise for reducing correctional officer stress, reducing agency cost and improving public safety. Agency administrators can construct the most effective program for their agencies by tailoring various program elements to their needs.

ENDNOTES

[1] This article is based on: National Institute of Justice. 2005. *Research for practice: Stress among probation and parole officers and what can be done about it.* Washington, D.C.: U.S. Department of Justice, Office of Justice Programs, National Institute of Justice. (June). Available at www.ncjrs.gov/pdffiles1/nij/205620.pdf.

The above research practice is based on an unpublished final report to the National Institute of Justice: Finn, P. and S. Kuck. 2003. *Addressing probation and parole officer stress.* Washington, D.C.: U.S. Department of Justice, National Institute of Justice. Available at www.ncjrs.gov/pdffiles1/nij/grants/207012.pdf.

[2] National Institute of Justice. 2005.

[3] Faulkner, Richard (Correctional Program Specialist, National Institute of Corrections), personal communication with authors of the NIJ Research for Practice.

Brown, P.W. and M.J. Maggio. 1997. The evolution of officer safety training in the federal probation and pretrial services system. *Federal Probation,* 61(4):26-32.

[4] Simmons, C., J.K. Cochran and W.R. Blount. 1997. Effects of job-related stress and job satisfaction on probation officers' inclinations to quit. *American Journal of Criminal Justice,* 21(2):213-229.

This figure is far higher than among U.S. employees in general, one-third of whom rate their boss as unfair. Source: *The Hudson Employment Index,*

1(4):2. Retrieved April 2004 from www.hudson-index.com.

[5] This figure is comparable to firefighters' median annual salary of $36,233. However, it is lower than the $42,270 median annual salary of police and sheriff's patrol officers.

Figures are from: Bureau of Labor Statistics, U.S. Department of Labor. 2000. *Occupational Outlook Handbook, 2000-01 edition* (bulletin 2520). Washington, D.C.: Superintendent of Documents, U.S. Government Printing Office.

[6] Figures are from: Bureau of Labor Statistics. *Occupational outlook handbook, 2006-07 edition.* Washington, D.C.: U.S. Department of Labor, Bureau of Labor Statistics. Available at www.bls.gov/oco/ocos265.htm.

[7] See the questionnaire used in an NIJ-sponsored survey of stress among police officers: Finn, P. and S. Kuck. 2003. Appendix F.

[8] National Institute of Justice. 2005.

ADDITIONAL READING

Finn, P. and J. Esselman Tomz. 1997. *Developing a law enforcement stress program for officers and their families.* Washington, D.C.: U.S. Department of Justice, National Institute of Justice. Available at www.ncjrs.gov/pdffiles/163175.pdf.

Finn, P. 2000. *Addressing correctional officer stress: Programs and strategies.* Washington, D.C.: U.S. Department of Justice, National Institute of Justice and Corrections Program Office. Available at www.ncjrs.gov/pdffiles1/nij/183474.pdf.

Duress Systems in Correctional Facilities

By National Institute of Justice Staff

Duress systems can help correctional officers respond quickly and effectively to the many dangers they face while performing their jobs. Consider this scenario: While on routine patrol, a correctional officer opens a cell door to check on the inmate slumped over inside. Suddenly, the inmate lunges at the unarmed officer, knocks him down and stabs him with a crude handmade knife. The only witnesses to the violent attack are other inmates who, even if they want to, can do nothing to help. Fortunately, if his facility uses a duress system, the officer can trigger a transmitter on his belt that can send a "man down" alarm and summon aid.

What Is a Duress System?

To respond effectively to assaults on personnel and other emergencies, correctional facilities must be able to pinpoint the location and nature of the problem within seconds of its occurrence. A duress system is typically composed of a closed network of portable and mounted transmitters and receivers linked by ultrasonic, infrared or radio frequency waves to a command center alarm console. It permits the rapid and coordinated response that can save lives and reduce institutional damage.

Background

The National Institute of Justice and the U.S. Department of Defense work together on projects involving the development and demonstration of emerging technologies of mutual interest and benefit to the military, corrections and law enforcement communities. The Staff Alarm and Inmate Tracking (SAINT) program, which operates at the Navy's Space and Naval Warfare (SPAWAR) Systems Center in Charleston, S.C., is one such joint venture. SAINT researches systems for use in correctional facilities and provides guidelines for acquiring and implementing such technologies. The program promotes safety for both correctional officers and inmates through the use of alarm systems.

As part of the project, SPAWAR developed the *Correctional Officer Duress Systems: Selection Guide,* which is intended to help with the identification, selection and deployment of this technology. It provides detailed information on nine commercially available systems, covering the alarm, locator and control subsystems; hardware/software used; and additional features. The guide also provides contact information for system vendors, so administrators can follow up with requests for additional information.

Types of Duress Systems

Three types of alarm systems are available for commercial sale, each designed to fulfill different needs and varying in its limitations.

Type I: Panic Button Alarm. These basic systems use buttons located on walls, underneath desks and near doorways. Pushing a button transmits a dedicated signal to a central alarm console. Using visible and/or audible enunciations, the alarm console identifies the location of the event where the alarm was triggered. Type I systems are simple, effective for many types of emergencies, relatively inexpensive and easy to install.

Type II: Identification Alarm. In Type II systems, portable transmitters broadcast a wireless signal to a nearby sensor, which forwards the alarm to a central console. The alarm signal includes an identification code that tells the dispatcher who sounded the alarm. Because officers carry these transmitters with them, they can sound an alarm from almost anywhere within a facility. Use of a Type II system also eliminates most false alarms.

Type III: Identification/Location Alarm. Type III systems operate much like Type II systems, with the added feature of tracking correctional facility staff members and pinpointing the alarm location. An extensive wireless infrastructure identifies, localizes and tracks the transmitting device. The system may produce a positioning symbol on a console panel or a map-like display at a central alarm location.

The limitations of each system vary:

- Type I systems may be inaccessible in a duress situation because they are mounted in fixed locations. They also lend themselves to false alarms triggered by inmates;
- Type II systems cannot localize alarms within a facility; and
- Type III systems are more expensive than other systems and are the most difficult to install.

System Selection

Selecting an appropriate officer duress system for a particular facility requires those involved in the selection process to define their own specific requirements and needs. Administrators might consider the following factors when choosing a system:

Cost. How much does it cost to install and integrate the system? What are the expected operational and maintenance costs?

Scalability/Flexibility. Can the system be expanded and updated as needed?

Installation and Integration. Is the installation process simple? Will the duress system integrate smoothly and successfully with other systems already in operation?

Reliability. Does the system self-test for accuracy? Does it have a battery backup in case of power failure? Do the transmitters indicate when batteries are low? Is maintenance readily available?

Operator Usage. Is it easy to learn how the system works? What about ease of day-to-day use?

Coverage. Given the design quirks and flaws of a particular facility, how complete will coverage be?

Outlook

Vendors are working on systems that will use emerging technologies, such as global positioning systems; ultra wideband (a radio frequency-based technology that operates across a broad frequency range at low power levels, emitting short pulses that exhibit a wide spectrum); and biometrics, which is the science of positive identification using an individual's unique characteristics such as facial features, fingerprints, voice and eyes. Each technology, however, has distinct advantages and disadvantages that have to be considered regarding incorporation into a duress system.

This article is based on NIJ's publication, In Short: Duress Systems in Corrections Facilities, which is available at www.ncjrs.gov/pdffiles1/nij/205836.pdf. Also see the full report, Correctional Officer Duress Systems: Selection Guide, at www.ncjrs.gov/pdffiles1/nij/ grants/202947.pdf.

Reprinted with permission of the American Correctional Association, Corrections Today, June 2006.

NIJ Update

No More "Cell" Phones

By National Institute of Justice Staff

Editor's Note: *This article was reprinted from the Winter 2005 edition of TechBeat, the quarterly news magazine of the National Law Enforcement and Corrections Technology Center, an NIJ program. Analyses of test results do not represent product approval or endorsement by the National Institute of Justice, U.S. Department of Justice; the National Institute of Standards and Technology, U.S. Department of Commerce; or Aspen Systems Corp. Points of view or opinions contained in this document are those of the authors and do not necessarily represent the official position or policies of the U.S. Department of Justice.*

In the late-night quiet of a prison cellblock, an inmate slips his hand into a small slit under his mattress and pulls out a cell phone. Speed dial connects him to his outside contact, he speaks a few prearranged words, and another drug deal is made. Technology allows him to operate as if he were still on the streets.

As cell phones become smaller, it becomes easier to smuggle them inside correctional facilities and easier for inmates to continue their criminal activities, harass victims or transmit photographs of information.

Fortunately, in today's technology-driven society, when one innovation creates a problem, a new one usually comes along to solve it. But, for corrections the question becomes where to find the right innovation.

Several possible technology approaches have been identified to deal with the cell phone problem in prisons and correctional facilities:

Locate and confiscate cell phones. This approach, says Ike Eichenlaub, chief of the Federal Bureau of Prisons' Office of Security Technology, requires a technology that minimally will:

- Work even when cell phones are turned on for only a few minutes at a time;
- Detect signals coming from any area of a facility; and
- Find transmissions through thick concrete walls in single story to multifloored buildings and in locations from urban areas to remote rural districts.

Ideally, he says, such technology would require minimal or no training to use, expand to cover other wireless technologies such as two-way pagers and operate on a 24/7 basis.

Overpower the signal with a stronger signal. "Another potential approach is commonly referred to as 'jamming,' which emits a signal stronger than a cell phone's signal and renders it useless," Eichenlaub says. Senior BOP Technologist Jim Mahan adds, "There are two types. One is called brute force jamming, which just blocks everything. The problem is, it's like power-washing the airwaves, and it bleeds over into the public broadcast area. The other type puts out a small amount of interference, and you could potentially confine it within a single cellblock. You could use lots of little pockets of small jamming to keep a facility under control."

"Trick" the phone. Eichenlaub describes a third possible approach, commonly called "spoofing," as tricking the cell phone to react as if a "no service" signal is received.

The Federal Communications Commission, however, prohibits both jamming and spoofing, he says, so implementing either of these technologies would require legal and regulatory changes.

Intercept the signal. A fourth possible approach, signal interception, retrieves telephone and serial numbers from operational phones, but can be implemented only under a judge's order.

Eichenlaub says that although signal interception is feasible, "We are looking for the simplest option, which is signal detection. There are no regulatory or legal issues here; if you can find it, you can go get it."

Cellular providers use different communications protocols, but all cell phones use radio frequency (RF) antenna power. The BOP has studied a number of off-the-shelf technologies to detect RF signals. Although detection equipment is available, costs can reach tens of thousands of dollars. "Some work better than others," Mahan adds. "Some work for only a short distance, maybe about 15 to 20 feet. This is impractical if you're trying to cover 50 acres. Also, each device may cost about $1,000. There is some promising new technology that is showing better results than anything else we've ever seen, but they are still prototypes. The question is whether the technology can be made at a cost that we can afford."

In response, BOP, the National Institute of Justice (NIJ), and the Naval Surface Warfare Center–Dahlgren are collaborating on a multiyear project to evaluate the problem and ultimately help develop that technology. BOP spent the first 6 months of 2004 evaluating and testing various possibilities. Now Dahlgren staff members (with NIJ funding) will evaluate the problem and potential technical solutions to provide a roadmap for addressing it. In the course of this evaluation, they will:

- Analyze and document BOP's work;
- Discuss this issue with the American Correctional Association and the Association of State Correctional Administrators to ascertain the needs of state and local correctional institutions and determine how they might differ from BOP requirements;
- Assess the spectrum of potential approaches and technology solutions; and
- Ultimately, incorporate BOP's work and other information into a report that recommends NIJ's next technology development steps.

Gary Maclellan, project manager for NIJ, expects the report to be released in FY 2006. For more information on the BOP's research into cell phone use by inmates, contact Ike Eichenlaub at (202) 305-8448 or LEichenlaub@ bop.gov. For more information on NIJ's involvement, contact Gary Maclellan at (202) 305-7339 or Gary.Maclellan @usdoj.gov.

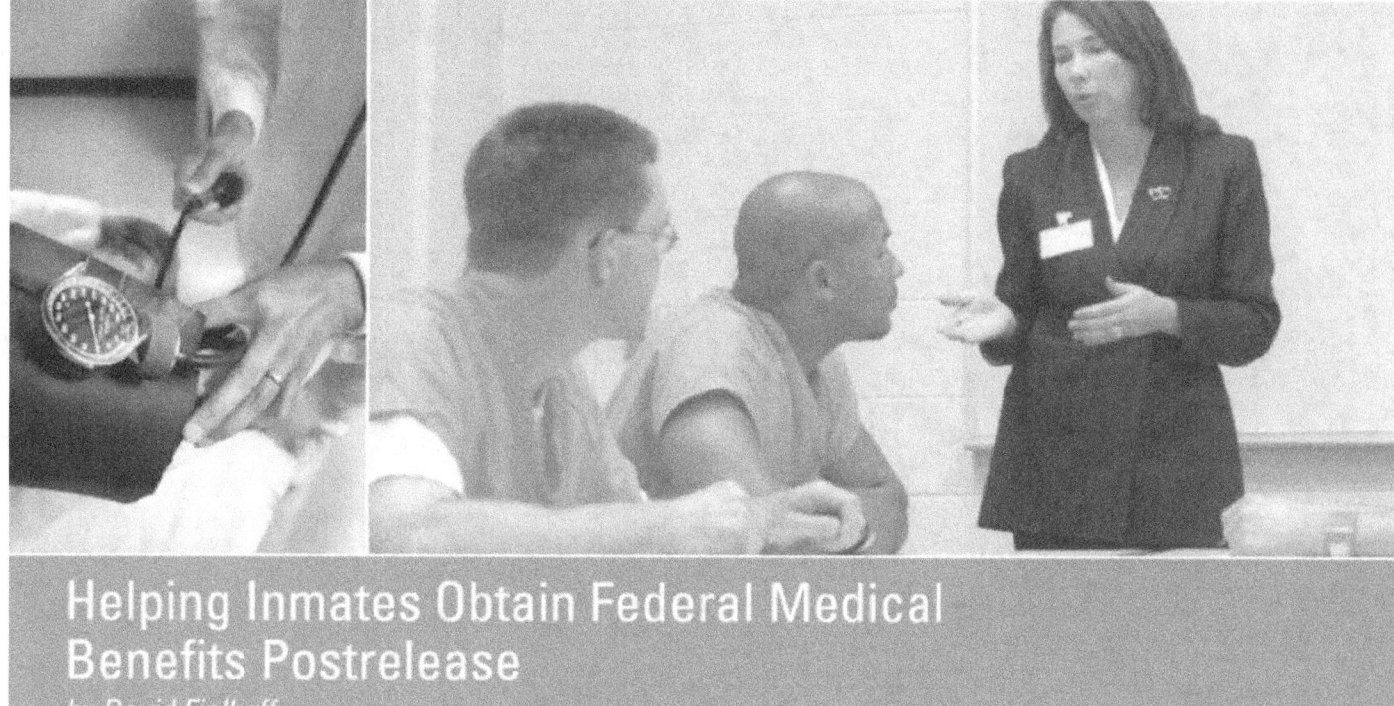

Helping Inmates Obtain Federal Medical Benefits Postrelease
by David Fialkoff

About the Author
Mr. Fialkoff is a senior writer/editor with the National Criminal Justice Reference Service.

Thousands of ill or disabled inmates are incarcerated in Federal, State, and local correctional facilities across the United States. The challenge of helping them obtain medical treatment and services after they are released is not a new one, but a recently released report looks at three programs that are assisting inmates in applying for such benefits.

Helping Inmates Obtain Federal Disability Benefits: Serious Medical and Mental Illness, Incarceration, and Federal Disability Entitlement Programs—cosponsored by the National Institute of Justice (NIJ) and the Centers for Disease Control and Prevention—reveals that many experts believe that continuing treatment after inmates are released results in a more successful return to society and could prevent the spread of tuberculosis,

hepatitis C, HIV/AIDS, and drug-resistant strains of viruses, thus minimizing the cost to community and corrections health care systems. It also could reduce crime—and hence recidivism—by releasees who continue to receive the medical and mental health treatment they need.

Federal disability benefits—Medicaid, Social Security Disability Insurance (SSDI), Supplemental Security Insurance (SSI), and veterans' compensation funds—offer one solution. Unfortunately, as many officials know, the process of applying for Federal benefits is often complex, and incarceration makes it difficult for inmates to collect their medical information. Three programs investigated in the NIJ study demonstrate, however, that assisting severely ill inmates with applying for these benefits before they leave prison may dramatically increase their chances of receiving benefits postrelease and ease their transition back into the community.

Three Benefits Assistance Programs

The study looked at benefits assistance programs in three jurisdictions:

- **Philadelphia.** The Coordinating Office for Drug and Alcohol Programs, part of the Philadelphia Behavioral Health System, offers services in behavioral health, case management, and job training to inmates through the Forensic Intensive Recovery Program.

- **New York.** Through a memorandum of understanding with the New York State Division of Parole, the Social Security Administration helps inmates apply, prior to their release, for SSI and SSDI benefits.

- **Texas.** The Texas Correctional Office on Offenders with Medical or Mental Impairments assists inmates who are elderly, terminally ill, mentally ill or disabled, or physically or developmentally disabled. Along with other State and local entities, the Office funds transitional, case management, and medical support for these individuals.

Recommendations for Implementing Programs

Recognizing the challenges of discharge planning for severely ill inmates, the researchers offered six recommendations for agencies that want to implement similar programs:

1. **Partnerships keep the process alive.** Whether a benefits applications process operates through a formal interagency agreement (as in Texas and New York) or an informal accord (as in Philadelphia), inmates receive better assistance when many agencies, organizations, and individuals work together to ensure that applications do not fall through the cracks and that benefits are distributed.

2. **Dedicated staff is important.** Specialized staff members who help offenders access benefits can streamline the

Many experts believe that continuing treatment after inmates are released results in a more successful return to society and could prevent the spread of tuberculosis, hepatitis C, HIV/AIDS, and drug-resistant strains of viruses, thus minimizing the cost to community and corrections health care systems.

process, provide complete applications for more individuals, and establish stronger working relationships with disability decisionmakers. In Texas, for example, the primary burden of gathering medical and mental health documentation shifted from corrections medical staff to benefits eligibility specialists, resulting in medical staff becoming more willing to assist in preparing applications.

3. **Filling the gaps until benefits commence is essential.** The benefits for many severely ill inmates do not begin immediately upon release. The Texas and Philadelphia programs pay for services during the period between an inmate's release and the start of disability or health benefits.

4. **Tracking outcomes is beneficial.** Collecting outcome data on the benefits process allows staff to evaluate the progress of the program and garner additional financial support to offset costs. For example, the Texas program assesses which eligibility specialists were successful in obtaining benefits for inmates, and then uses these assessments in staff training. In contrast, New York does not maintain data on Social Security applications, so staff members in that program often assumed their efforts were largely unsuccessful, making it difficult for them to feel motivated when filing applications.

5. **Centralizing operations reduces delays and improves communication.** All three sites discovered the benefits of centralizing the medical and cash assistance claims processes. Philadelphia's use of partnerships in the medical assistance applications process reduced the number of people involved in decisionmaking and significantly reduced the time until enrollment began.

6. **Assisting mentally ill offenders poses special challenges.** Some individuals interviewed for the study suggested that disability-determination staff appeared to be more cautious when approving benefits for mentally ill inmates. A number of complex situations may account for this: Offenders also may suffer from substance abuse, which can make it difficult to determine the primary illness; offenders may feign mental illness to obtain more favorable treatment; and truly mentally ill offenders may appear more stable within the structured environment of prison.

Benefits Are Only One Aspect of Planning

Helping inmates apply for medical and cash assistance is an important way to support the return of severely ill inmates to the community, according to the report. The researchers recommended, however, that such assistance should be part of a more extensive discharge plan that includes case management and housing services.

NCJ 218266

For More Information

- Conly, C.H., *Helping Inmates Obtain Federal Disability Benefits: Serious Medical and Mental Illness, Incarceration and Federal Disability Entitlement Programs*, final report submitted to the National Institute of Justice, Washington, DC: Abt Associates Inc., November 2005 (NCJ 211989), available at www.ncjrs.gov/pdffiles1/nij/grants/211989.pdf.

Publications in Brief

Social Science Computer Review: Symposium on Crime Mapping

Ronald Wilson, ed.
Volume 25, No. 2, Summer 2007

Crime mapping continues to help criminal justice practitioners and researchers perform higher quality, more efficient, more responsive work. Geographic information systems (GIS) and spatial data analysis techniques are well-established tools for analyzing criminal behavior and its effect on the criminal justice system and society.

In a special issue of the *Social Science Computer Review*, experts discuss the history of crime mapping and the software advancements that shape the current field. Edited by Ronald Wilson, program manager of the National Institute of

Justice's Mapping and Analysis for Public Safety Program and Data Resources, this journal issue explores the "automation of geography" through software and how it enables law enforcement to better understand the spatial elements of crime.

Topics include the use of GIS and other spatial analysis software programs to:
- Visualize the distribution of sex offenders.
- Study crime around substance abuse treatment centers.
- Examine the travel patterns of bank robbers.
- Explore local crime patterns in urban areas.

For more information, visit http://hcl.chass. ncsu.edu/sscore/sscore.htm.

Obtaining Federal Benefits for Disabled Offenders:

Part 1 — Social Security Benefits

By Marilyn Moses and
Roberto Hugh Potter

Authors' note: Points of view expressed in this article do not represent the official position or policies of the U.S. Department of Justice.

The typical offender reentry plan involves, at a minimum, efforts to help the offender secure a job, find affordable and safe housing, and comply with other conditions of release. But reentry plans for offenders who have special needs — who are mentally ill or have HIV/AIDS, for example — can be far more complex.

Corrections staff in most facilities do not typically help inmates apply for federal entitlement programs like Social Security and Medicaid as part of reentry planning. For severely ill inmates, discharge planning that includes assistance in applying for federal disability benefits is still more the exception than the rule.

To understand more about how to plan for reentry of special needs offenders, health care providers and corrections administrators approached the National Institute of Justice (NIJ) and the Centers for Disease Control and Prevention (CDC) to learn about disability benefits and the efficacy of efforts to obtain disability entitlements for soon-to-be-released offenders.

This month's NIJ Update is the first of several that discuss findings from the NIJ/CDC co-funded research. This article describes the results of efforts in Texas and New York to release offenders from prison with social security benefits. Next month's column will describe research that examined the effectiveness of Medicaid in keeping offenders from returning to jail.

The Bottom Line

The sites involved in the NIJ/CDC study maintain that helping offenders obtain federal disability benefits not only can increase their access to community-based care, it can also: 1) reduce the financial burden on state and local governments that fund indigent health care systems and 2) increase the number of disabled offenders who receive treatment. However, the challenges are significant: The process takes a long time; it can be confusing; and there is no guarantee an offender will qualify for benefits.

Obtaining federal disability benefits should be viewed as only one facet of a much broader discharge plan. Even releasees who ultimately qualify for and receive benefits are likely to find it challenging to avoid relapse or recidivism, unless other supports, such as case management services and housing are made available.

Overview

The Social Security Administration administers two programs that provide monthly cash benefits to disabled people who meet certain criteria. The two programs are Retirement, Survivors, and Disability Insurance, commonly referred to as Social Security Disability Insurance (SSDI), and Supplemental Security Income (SSI).

People who acquire a disabling impairment while committing a felony are barred for life from receiving SSDI and SSI benefits based on that impairment, although they may have other impairments that qualify them for benefits. In addition, federal law prohibits payment of benefits to applicants if drug or alcohol abuse is the sole or primary diagnosis.

Social Security Disability Insurance. To qualify for SSDI, an applicant must meet certain nonmedical criteria and must be found to have a physical or mental impairment that either has lasted, or is expected to last, for at least a year or will result in death. The impairment must be so severe that the individual cannot engage in substantial gainful employment. The amount of a person's SSDI payment varies according to how much the person contributed to social security while employed.

Supplemental Security Income. Unlike SSDI, SSI is a means-tested entitlement that is financed, not through worker contributions, but through general tax revenues. It is available to aged, blind or disabled people who have limited assets and income. Recipients must be U.S. citizens or "qualified aliens."[1] Because SSI is considered a benefit of last resort, applicants must agree to apply for all other cash benefits to which they may be entitled (such as pensions, veterans benefits, SSDI) before they receive SSI.

Eligibility. Determining eligibility for SSI and SSDI involves taking several sequential steps that take from 90 to 120 days to complete. The Social Security Administration must determine an inmate's medical and nonmedical eligibility status based on a number of criteria.[2] If an inmate's disability is denied, as are the majority of first-time claims, and appeals are filed, the process can be significantly longer than 120 days. It can take several years in some cases.

Effects of Incarceration on Eligibility for Benefits. People who are receiving SSDI or SSI benefits have their benefits suspended if they are incarcerated for more than 30 days. SSDI benefits are restored upon release if the person files a request

with the Social Security Administration. People who are receiving SSI benefits when they are incarcerated will have their benefits terminated if they are incarcerated for 12 consecutive months. They must reapply and resubmit their application and records upon release in order to regain their benefits.

Texas' Experience

The Texas Correctional Office on Offenders with Medical and Mental Impairments (TCOOMMI) offers institutional and community-based services to juvenile and adult offenders with special needs, including those with mental illness, mental retardation or terminal illness.

Although the Social Security Administration allows residents of public institutions to apply for benefits before they are released, submitting applications early in Texas was typically limited to the few inmates whose work histories allowed them to apply for SSDI or whose illnesses were terminal. Waiting to apply until the inmate was released generally resulted in a three- to four-month delay before inmates knew if their applications were approved. Releasees with severe mental illness were especially vulnerable during this period, frequently failing to stabilize in the community when they lacked an income and medical assistance.

Believing strongly that inmates who received medical and cash assistance shortly after release would be less likely to require emergency hospitalization or commit new crimes to obtain income, the TCOOMMI staff approached the Texas Legislature for authorization to launch a program to aid inmates with benefits applications prior to release. In 1999, the Legislature authorized a pilot project that lets TCOOMMI process inmates' prerelease applications 90 days before an inmate is scheduled to be released and allows inmates to receive medical approval of their applications before they are released.

The pilot project targets adult inmates with special needs. Twelve full- or part-time benefits eligibility specialists assist inmates eligible for benefits. Up to 120 days prior to an inmates' projected release date,

the staff contact the Social Security Administration to verify the inmate's current benefits status and begin meeting with the inmate to determine if he or she will have difficulty finding and keeping a job. Staff receive the inmate's permission to initiate the benefits application and obtain necessary signatures to release information. The eligibility specialists file the paperwork, track decisions and keep the Social Security Administration informed regarding the inmate's release status. When inmates are released, their files are transferred to the state or local mental health or human services agency nearest to their residence. In most cases, an eligibility specialist or caseworker at that location continues monitoring the offender's application.

Effects of The Texas Project

Texas' data show that the pilot project has succeeded in helping inmates obtain social security benefits, but the task is challenging. Of 1,686 individuals referred to benefits eligibility specialists in the first nine months of fiscal year 2002, 1,076 (64 percent) did not submit applications to the Social Security Administration. Most of the inmates who were referred but did not apply, refused to apply; reportedly, some believed they were capable of working, others did not feel they were ill enough to warrant receiving benefits and still others did not want the perceived stigma of being welfare recipients. However, once they were released, many applied for benefits because they realized that their expectations were unrealistic or their views were naïve. Unfortunately, they had lost precious time and money because of the delay.

Of the 610 individuals who did apply for benefits, 49 percent were approved, 38 percent were denied, and 13 percent were awaiting a decision at the time the data was collected. The data also revealed that the success rate for applications varied among benefits eligibility specialists. One specialist had a 92-percent approval rating. The keys to his success seemed to have been his attention to detail, ability to obtain

supporting medical examinations or documentation, and responsiveness to requests for additional information.

New York's Experience

New York, like Texas, has established a memorandum of understanding with the Social Security Administration to file prerelease applications for severely mentally and medically ill inmates housed in state prisons. New York's division of parole estimates that between 200 and 400 prerelease applications are submitted annually; about 31 percent of these initial claims for SSI are approved. The State Division of Disability Determination reports that it only initially approves 38 percent of claims from the nonincarcerated applicants statewide.

In New York, common reasons inmate claims are denied include:

- Applicants do not maintain contact (e.g., they move or fail to appear before their parole officer);
- Applicants are not qualified aliens;
- Medical records are not complete enough to determine disability. (Many inmates cannot remember their medical or mental health histories and do not have their records.); and
- Applicants whose initial claims are denied may refuse to appeal, preferring instead to apply for state-funded public assistance, which is available to some people who have been denied SSI.

The New York Division of Parole is working to improve its initial claim approval rate by addressing some of these issues. It has sent out written directives to all institutional and field agents re-emphasizing the importance of the prerelease application process. In addition, it has designated staff in its central office to assist the Social Security Administration with location issues and is developing medical and mental health protocols for prison staff to ensure that examinations and the corresponding documentation meet the requirements of the State's Division of Disability Determination.

Summary

Filing applications prior to release means more inmates now have benefits when they leave institutions. Having dedicated eligibility specialists prepare applications and gather medical records has reduced the burden on prison medical staff that once had sole responsibility for preparing the applications and sometimes felt overwhelmed at having benefits tasks added to their numerous treatment responsibilities.[3]

ENDNOTES

[1] For more information about the term "qualified alien," see Social Security Administration. 2002. *Understanding Supplemental Security Income.* Washington, D.C.: Social Security Administration. Available online at www.socialsecurity.gov/notices/supplemental securityincome/textunderstanding ssi.htm.

[2] See *How to Apply for Social Security Disability Benefits* on the Social Security Administration Web site. Available online at www. ssa.gov/disability.html.

[3] For more information about the benefits programs described in this article, see Conly, Catherine H. 2005. *Helping inmates obtain federal disability benefits: Serious medical and mental illness, incarceration, and federal disability entitlement programs.* Final Report for contract no. 99-C-008 2002TO097 000. Washington D.C.: U.S. Department of Justice, National Institute of Justice. (June). Available online at www.ncjrs.gov/pdffiles1/nij/grants/211989.pdf.

Marilyn Moses is a social science analyst for the National Institute of Justice, Office of Justice Programs, U.S. Department of Justice. Roberto Hugh Potter is a public health advisor at the Centers for Disease Control and Prevention, U.S. Department of Health and Human Services.

Obtaining Federal Benefits for Disabled Offenders:

Part 2 — Medicaid Benefits

By Marilyn Moses and R. Hugh Potter

Authors' note: Findings and conclusions reported in this article are those of the authors and do not necessarily represent the official position or policies of the U.S. departments of Justice and Health and Human Services.

This month's column is the second of three articles about findings from research funded by the National Institute of Justice (NIJ), the Centers for Disease Control and Prevention (CDC), the National Institute of Mental Health, and the John D. and Catherine T. MacArthur Foundation's Mental Health Policy Research Network. Part 1 described research about obtaining social security benefits. Part 2 describes research about the likelihood of losing Medicaid benefits as a result of being jailed and the value of having Medicaid benefits upon release.

NIJ and CDC have co-funded research on how various correctional systems help offenders obtain federal disability benefits before they are released. Sites involved in this study assert that helping offenders obtain disability benefits prior to release from jail or prison not only can increase their access to community-based care, it can also: 1) reduce the financial burden on state and local governments that fund indigent health care systems, and 2) increase the number of disabled offenders who receive treatment. A follow-up study conducted in two jails, funded by NIJ, the John D. and Catherine T. MacArthur Foundation's Mental Health Policy Research Network, and the National Institute of Mental Health, supports these beliefs.

But the challenges are significant: The process takes a long time; it can be confusing; and there is no guarantee an offender will qualify for benefits. Researchers point out that obtaining federal disability benefits should be viewed as only one facet of a much broader discharge plan. Even releasees who ultimately qualify for and receive benefits are likely to find it challenging to avoid relapse or recidivism unless other supports, such as case management services and housing, are made available.

Overview of Medicaid

Medicaid is a means-tested entitlement program that provides medical insurance to low-income people. It is jointly funded by federal and state governments based on a formula that results in considerable variation in Medicaid coverage across states. Although there are a number of ways to qualify for Medicaid, most people do so by qualifying for Supplemental Security Income (SSI) from the Social Security Administration (SSA).[1]

Disabled people who receive Medicaid have a wide range of physical and mental conditions, but Medicaid coverage does not extend to drug and alcohol addiction. Most states terminate Medicaid eligibility for people who are incarcerated. A few states have found ways to ensure that Medicaid benefits begin again as soon as possible after the inmate is released.

Experiences in Two Jails

Concern has been expressed by advocacy groups that access to treatment and continuity of care is seriously compromised by the current Medicaid disenrollment policy for jail detainees with serious mental illness. The concern stems from the SSA's enforcement of its inmate exclusion rule — if an individual is incarcerated for one full calendar month, benefits will be suspended. In most states, Medicaid enrollment is tied to SSA disability benefits. Hence, if a detainee is cut off from SSA benefits, he or she, in turn, also loses Medicaid benefits. Once released, the individual can apply for benefit reinstatement, but the process to reinstate benefits is a lengthy one and can take as long as three months. Despite the concerns of advocates, research findings suggest that benefits often are reinstated upon release.

In King County, Wash., and Pinellas County, Fla., researchers found that jailed disability benefits recipients were not incarcerated long enough to lose their SSA or Medicaid disability benefits. Detainees in the King County and Pinellas County study spent an average of 16 to 30 days in jail, so virtually all of those with severe mental illness who had Medicaid at jail entry (about 65 to 78 percent in the two counties) also had it upon release. In both counties only 3 percent of detainees were incarcerated long enough for their benefits to be suspended. Stated another away, 97 percent of the detainees who were receiving Medicaid benefits when jailed retained their disability benefits upon release.[2]

Researchers also found that having Medicaid benefits at the time of release from jail appeared to help detainees with severe mental illness from returning to jail in the year following their release. In both counties, detainees with severe mental illness who had Medicaid when they were released, had about 16 percent fewer detentions than similar detainees with no Medicaid benefits. Releasees with Medicaid benefits had an average of 1.9 detentions. Releasees with no Medicaid benefits had an average of 2.3 detentions. Detainees with severe mental illness and who had Medicaid upon release from jail were also more likely to access community treatment services, receive services more quickly and receive more services than matched detainees without Medicaid in a 90-day post-release study period.

Detainees in Pinellas County released with Medicaid were 1.6 times

Continued on page 78

NIJ Update

Continued from page 76

more likely than non-Medicaid releasees to access community treatment services within 90 days post-release. Releasees in King County who had Medicaid when released were 1.25 times as likely to access services. Releasees with Medicaid in both counties also received services more quickly than those without this disability benefit. In Pinellas County, the first treatment service contact took place in about three weeks (21.7 days) as compared to four weeks (28.5 days) for non-Medicaid releasees. The results were similar for King County — about two weeks (13.5 days) to first service contact for Medicaid recipients and almost 19 days for those without Medicaid benefits. In both counties, releasees with Medicaid also received more services than those without this benefit. Releasees with Medicaid in Pinellas County received 7.5 days of service compared to 4.5 days for those without Medicaid. In King County, Medicaid releasees received 11 days vs. seven days for non-Medicaid releasees.

Having Medicaid also appeared to help severely mentally ill releasees in King County stay longer in the community before their next detention. Those with Medicaid stayed in the community an average of 102 days vs. 93 days for those without Medicaid. In Pinellas County, having access to Medicaid had no effect.[3] These limited research findings appear promising even though they involve only two counties and only offenders with severe mental illness in jail who are eligible for Medicaid. Results may vary for other communities if jail stays consistently exceed the 30-day Medicaid cut-off and if, as a result, Medicaid benefits are suspended at much higher rates. Results also do not apply to the many mentally ill offenders in jail who have less serious psychiatric diagnoses or people who might receive a diagnosis representing severe mental illness if seen by a psychiatrist, but who were either not enrolled in Medicaid or not known to the public mental health system at the time of the study.

Findings

What is generalizable from the data from King County and Pinellas County is that it is not likely that a seriously mentally ill jailed Medicaid recipient will have his or her benefits suspended when jailed due to the fact that individuals are not usually detained long enough for benefits to be suspended. Severely mentally ill offenders who are released with Medicaid are more likely to access community treatment services, to receive services more quickly and to receive more days of service than those without Medicaid. They are also less likely to return to jail and more likely to stay out of jail for longer periods of time than non-Medicaid releasees.

What is not generalizable to prisons is the high rate of Medicaid enrollment at release for detainees with severe mental illness. Prisons are long-stay institutions (the average length of incarceration is more than five years), so 100 percent of those who enter prison with Medicaid lose it before they are released. The same is true for SSI benefits and other entitlements. State prisoners with severe mental illness need the same access to equally intensive evidence-based treatments as jail detainees.

Whether talking about jails or prisons, however, it is the quality of treatment services that is likely to make a difference in the ability of severely mentally ill offenders to function in the community and avoid recidivism. Simply diverting people with severe mental illness to everyday or generic mental health services in the community is unlikely to have a positive impact on their ability to live in the community free of criminal justice entanglements.[4]

Generic services are not intensive enough nor are they attuned enough to the multiple comorbidities of severely mentally ill offenders. What is needed is diversion to intensive services such as assertive community treatment or dual diagnosis treatment teams, which have an evidence base and proven track record of being successful in treating persons with severe mental illness. Evidence-based treatments that promote recovery and increase opportunities for successful community living offer the best hope for people with severe mental illnesses, whether they are released from prisons or jails. However, solid research data backing up this assessment for people with severe mental illness in jails or other correctional settings are not currently available. Responding to this gap in the current knowledge base should be a high priority for both the mental health and criminal justice research communities.

REFERENCES

[1] The Kaiser Commission on Medicaid and the Uninsured. 2001. *Medicaid's role for the disabled population under age 65*. Washington, D.C.: The Henry J. Kaiser Family Foundation. (April).

[2] Morrissey, J.P., K.M. Dalton, H.J. Steadman, G.S. Cuddeback, D. Haynes and A. Cuellar. 2006. Assessing Gaps between policy and practice in Medicaid disenrollment of jail detainees with severe mental illness. *Psychiatric Services*, 57(6):803-808.

[3] Morrissey, J.P., H.J. Steadman, K.M. Dalton, A. Cuellar, P. Stiles and G.S. Cuddeback. 2006. Medicaid enrollment and mental health service use following release of jail detainees with severe mental illness. *Psychiatric Services*, 57(6):809-815.

[4] Steadman, H. J. and M. Naples. 2005. Assessing the effectiveness of jail diversion programs for persons with serious mental illness and co-occurring substance use disorders. *Behavioral Sciences and the Law*, 23(2):163-170. Delmar, NY: Policy Research Associates.

For more information about the benefits programs described in this article, see:

• Conly, Catherine H. 2005. *Helping inmates obtain federal disability benefits: Serious medical and mental illness, incarceration, and federal disability entitlement programs*, Final report for contract no. 99-C-008 2002TO097 000, NCJ 211989. (June). Available at: http://www.ncjrs.gov/pdf-files1/ nij/grants/211989.pdf.

• Morrissey, Joseph P. 2006. *Medicaid benefits and recidivism of mentally ill persons released from jail*, Final report for award no. 2004M-051, NCJ 214169. (May).

For more information about the rules and regulations for federal benefits programs, contact your state and federal benefits agencies directly.

Marilyn Moses is a social science analyst for the National Institute of Justice, Office of Justice Programs, U.S. Department of Justice. R. Hugh Potter is a senior health scientist at the Centers for Disease Control and Prevention, U.S. Department of Health and Human Services.

NIJ Update

Obtaining Federal Benefits for Disabled Offenders:

Part 3 — The Challenges And Lessons Learned

By Marilyn Moses and R. Hugh Potter

Authors' Note: Findings and conclusions reported in this article are those of the authors and do not necessarily represent the official position or policies of the U.S. departments of Justice or Health and Human Services.

The previous two articles in this series discussed findings from Catherine H. Conly's *Helping Inmates Obtain Federal Disability Benefits: Serious Medical and Mental Illness, Incarceration, and Federal Disability Entitlement Programs*, a study about programs designed to obtain federal benefits for inmates as part of reentry planning. The research, jointly funded by the National Institute of Justice and the Centers for Disease Control and Prevention, showed that helping offenders obtain federal disability benefits not only can increase their access to community-based care, it can also: 1) reduce the financial burden on state and local governments that fund indigent health care systems, and 2) increase the number of disabled offenders who receive treatment.[1] This article summarizes what the researchers identified as the primary challenges to and lessons learned about obtaining benefits for offenders who are entitled to them.

Challenges

The programs the researchers studied face a number of common challenges to obtaining benefits:

Staff resistance. Some staff and professionals may resist helping inmates because they feel that offenders do not deserve this type of assistance. Because corrections staff, including contract medical and mental health staff, may not view benefits planning as part of their job duties, they may resist participating in the process because it places additional burdens on their time. Likewise, parole officers may not assign high priority to having parolees apply for or obtain benefits.

Applicant impairments. Illiteracy, language barriers, and mental and physical health conditions can make it difficult for severely ill offenders to participate effectively in the application process. Illness may also impair their memory of prior treatment.

Offender resistance. Inmates may refuse to participate in filling out prerelease applications for Supplemental Security Income (SSI) or Social Security Disability Insurance (SSDI) only to discover after release that they cannot support themselves or obtain care. Parolees who have obtained prerelease approval for benefits may not follow through with obtaining benefits after they are released.

Delay in determining disability. Even when applications for SSI or SSDI are filed before an inmate is released, the application review process can take a long time. As a result, benefits may not start for weeks or months after release.

High rates of denial for SSI. Initial SSI applications are often denied, which necessitates appeals that produce significant delays. If releasees do not have help filing appeals following release or cannot be located, they may lose the opportunity to obtain benefits.

Lack of information. Medical and mental health records necessary to substantiate the nature and duration of a disability may be difficult to obtain because offenders typically have seen multiple health care providers in the community. In addition, correctional records may be inaccurate or incomplete.

Inability to locate releasees. Even if they receive medical approval prior to release, releasees who cannot be located are likely to have their SSI or SSDI applications closed for lack of important information.

Lessons Learned

The experiences of the study sites suggest six important lessons regarding efforts to assist inmates with benefits applications:

1) Partnerships keep the process alive. Regardless of whether the benefits application process operates through a formal interagency agreement or an informal accord, inmates receive better assistance when many agencies, organizations and individuals work together to ensure that eligible applications do not fall through the cracks and that benefits are distributed.

2) Dedicating staff to the program has rewards. Specialized staff who help offenders access benefits can streamline the process, provide complete applications for more individuals and establish stronger working relationships with disability decision-makers. In Texas, for example, since the primary burden of gathering medical and mental health documentation shifted from medical staff to the benefits eligibility specialists, medical staff are more willing to assist in preparing applications.

3) Filling gaps until benefits commence is essential. The benefits for many severely ill inmates do not begin immediately upon release and programs may have to fill potential gaps in benefits by using their own program dollars to pay for services during the period between a client's release and the start of disability or health benefits.

4) Tracking outcomes is beneficial. Collecting outcome data on the benefits process not only allows staff to evaluate the progress of the program but also to garner additional financial support to offset costs. For example, in Texas, the staff assessed which eligibility specialists succeeded in obtaining benefits and used their techniques in staff training. In contrast, New York did not maintain data on social security applications, so its staff members often assumed their efforts were largely unsuccessful, making it difficult for them to feel motivated when filing applications.

5) Centralizing operations reduces delays and improves communication. Sites that centralized the medical and cash assistance claims process significantly reduced the amount of time until enrollment began.

6) Assisting mentally ill offenders poses special challenges. Some individuals interviewed for the research suggested that disability determination staff appear more cautious when approving benefits for mentally ill inmates. With fewer objective criteria, it is harder to diagnose a mental illness. In addition, there is a common perception that some offenders feign mental illness to obtain more favorable treatment or that those who are mentally ill can appear stable in the structured environment of a correctional setting. Some offenders also suffer from substance abuse, making it difficult to determine which ailment is the primary illness.

Benefits Are Just One Aspect of Planning

Helping inmates apply for medical and cash assistance is an important way to support severely ill inmates who are returning to the community. The study suggested, however, that such assistance should be viewed as only one facet of a more extensive discharge plan. Corrections staff should also provide case management and housing services. Even individuals who qualify for benefits may find it challenging to avoid relapse unless these supports are available

ENDNOTES

[1] The jurisdictions that participated in the research were the Texas Correctional Office on Offenders with Medical and Mental Impairments; the New York Division of Parole; the City of Philadelphia Behavioral Health System; King County, Wash.; and Pinellas County, Fla.

For more information about the benefits programs described in this article, see: Conly, Catherine H. 2005. *Helping inmates obtain federal disability benefits: Serious medical and mental illness, incarceration, and federal disability entitlement programs.* Final report for contract no. 99-C-008 2002TO097 000, NCJ 211989. (June). Available at http://www.ncjrs.gov/pdffiles1/nij/grants/211989.pdf

For more information about the rules and regulations for federal benefits programs, contact your state and federal benefits agencies directly.

Marilyn Moses is a social science analyst for the National Institute of Justice, Office of Justice Programs, U.S. Department of Justice. Roberto Hugh Potter is a senior health scientist at the Centers for Disease Control and Prevention, U.S. Department of Health and Human Services.

Faith-Based Programs Give Facilities a Helping Hand

By Laurie C. Bright and
Mary G. Graham

Authors' note: Findings and conclusions reported in this article are those of the authors and do not necessarily represent the official position or policies of the U.S. Department of Justice.

Religious groups have long played a role in helping prisoners and their families, and our nation's prisons have a considerable range of religion-based activities. At a minimum, every prison has at least one prison chaplain available,[1] and many prisons are offering more than prayer services or religious study. Increasingly, these programs offer in-prison, prerelease and reentry services to prisoners and their families. Corrections-related faith-based programs, staffed by committed volunteers, offer the potential to reduce the cost of providing services.

Research is inconclusive about the effectiveness of the programs in terms of their impact on recidivism or ability to change behavior, but some programs are building impressive track records and are helping correctional facilities provide much-needed services. This article highlights five of them.[2]

Marion, Ohio

The Horizon Program is a 48-bed unit for male inmates at the Marion Correctional Institution, which began operations in 2000. The program, which draws volunteers from the Christian, Jewish and Muslim faith communities in nearby Columbus, helps inmates develop pro-social beliefs and skills. Horizon at Marion has established strong partnerships with the faith community and taps into a remarkably stable pool of volunteers who provide spiritual development and mentoring activities. Each year, approximately 60 volunteers provide services in the Horizon unit. Only the program coordinator and volunteer coordinator are paid positions. The Marion Correctional Facility provides funding, and private sources such as churches also contribute, according to Program Coordinator Jeff Hunsaker.

Enlisting members of the community who can model pro-social behavior and attitudes is important in creating a change of heart in offenders and restoring them to better lives, Hunsaker said. Horizon targets inmates who have at least two years to serve before their release. This requirement gives inmates time to put into practice what they learn and to reduce behavioral problems while in prison. The selected inmates live in interfaith "families" for 10 months and receive spiritual mentoring as well as services to help change anti-social beliefs and behaviors, reunite with their families, gain basic life skills, and aid in recovery from addiction. Inmates are selected for the program after interviews with administrators and staff to gauge their readiness and commitment to changing their behavior. Last year, Horizon graduates were given the chance to recommend a fellow inmate to participate in the program. Correctional staff and program officials believe that inmates recommended by Horizon graduates could be successful candidates because the graduates would have insight into an inmate's willingness to change.

As of June 2006, Horizon at Marion had served 230 inmates; 179 have graduated and almost half — 86 — have been released. Of the 86, 14 percent have returned to the state prison system.[3] According to a Bureau of Justice Statistics report about U.S. reentry trends, 41 percent of inmates discharged by state parole authorities in 2000 successfully completed their supervision terms; 42 percent were returned to prison or jail; and 9 percent absconded.[4] In light of the national reentry trends, the Horizon program has shown a favorable recidivism rate.

Lawtey, Fla.

In 2001, Lawtey Correctional Institution established a faith- and character-based dormitory to house about 80 men; subsequently, it became the first institution of its kind in the country. Lawtey houses inmates in medium, minimum and community custody. To be selected, inmates must have had no disciplinary confinements within 90 days of application to Lawtey. Religious faith (or lack thereof) is not considered in the application process. The majority of the inmates report Christian affiliations; 4 percent are Muslim; and 1 percent are Jewish. Thirteen percent have no affiliation, and the remaining 5 percent belong to one of 10 other religions.

According to Senior Chaplain William Wright, approximately 600 volunteers have participated in programming at Lawtey, which offers services every day of the week. Inmates participate in a minimum of four hours a month of secular or faith-based self-improvement, including life skills training, mentoring and developing personal integrity. Wright said Lawtey routinely adds new programs to meet inmate needs. For example, Long Distance Dads was added to encourage inmate fathers to reunite with their children and stay involved in their lives, he said.

Program officials believe the atmosphere at Lawtey makes a difference. Inmates know they must "police themselves" and not engage in problem behavior such as fighting or stealing. Any inmate who has disciplinary problems is transferred to another facility. As a result, disciplinary problems at the facility declined to the point where confinement cells were shut down and staff transferred to other duties. In the six-month period ending May 31, 2007, Lawtey had a lower disciplinary rate per 1,000 than comparable Florida correctional institutions.[5]

According to a forthcoming evaluation report from the Urban Institute, at six months after release, male faith- and character-based institution (FCBI) inmates have lower reincarceration rates than a matched comparison group of inmates housed in the general population. None of the 189 male FCBI inmates included in the outcome analysis were reincarcerated within six months of their release, while four (2.1 percent) of the 189 male inmates in the matched comparison group were reincarcerated during that time, reported Nancy LaVigne, senior researcher at the Urban Institute in Washington, D.C.

Oregon

Home for Good Oregon (HGO) is a statewide community and faith-based reentry initiative involving a partnership between the Oregon Department of Corrections, local community corrections agencies, citizens, communities and faith-based groups in each of Oregon's 36 counties. Four counties — Marion, Linn, Douglas and Josephine — are serving as pilot projects, working with Partnership Steering Committees, which direct the development of volunteers, services and coordination. A network of nine full-time prison chaplains works in eight correctional institutions to help offenders develop spiritually and prepare for release in the last six months of their incarceration. In addition, 45 volunteer community chaplains, trained by the Department of Corrections, recruit and work with hundreds of community- and faith-based volunteers.

HGO has received more than 1,600 applications since September 2004 — about 280 per month. Offenders of all faiths are welcome. Applicants receive the name and contact information for a volunteer community chaplain in their county as well as two or more local community- or faith-based resources. In three counties, an effort called Circles of Support and Accountability (COSA) involves highly trained volunteers who meet weekly, giving high-risk offenders additional support and augmenting services provided by corrections professionals. The program is based on the restorative justice model, focusing on the

community. According to Thomas O'Connor, program administrator, volunteers who can model pro-social attitudes and behaviors can help motivate offenders to use available community resources for housing, employment training and other needs. "The community has a vital role in making the reentry process a successful process for both returning offenders and the communities receiving them," he said. At the time of this article, there are no data on the effect of the services provided,[6] but O'Connor says anecdotal evidence indicates that people who have community support have lower rates of failing to report to their parole officers.

East Harlem, N.Y.

In 1999, the Harlem Exodus Transitional Community (ETC) received $40,000 in contributions from a church and began providing services to inmates returning to the community. Since then, the program's annual budget has grown substantially, much of it from large grants from the federal government, Esperanza USA and several foundations. ETC received funds under Ready4Work, an ex-offender reentry work force development initiative of the U.S. Department of Labor's Center for Faith-Based and Community Initiatives. The Ready4Work funding required that the program not have an overt faith focus and participation in the program's spiritual components not be mandatory.

With the exception of sex offenders and those with mental illness, ETC serves all types of criminal offenders, including those with gang-related offenses and histories of violence. However, this community-based program has no formal affiliation with the correctional system. The program is staffed by professionals, many of whom are ex-offenders. Case managers act as mentors and partners. Each participant must have 10 contacts with a case manager in the first month, five in the second and two in the third. Participants can stay in the program for up to a year, with the number of contacts depending on how well they are doing. Volunteers from the faith community serve as life coach mentors and hold mentoring meetings once a week, but the

mentors and participants also meet at other times for guidance as well as friendship and conversation.

The ETC program serves 400 to 500 formerly incarcerated men and women a year. It focuses on employment counseling and training and helps participants build on the skills they acquired in correctional settings to secure positions outside prison. Following their initial five-day reintegration session, participants leave with a professional resume, interview skills and an understanding of the attitudes and habits they need in the workplace. The program's employment specialists reach out to employers in New York City to develop job opportunities for participants. Adam Friedman, deputy director of ETC, said some of the employers recently involved are the #311 information system in New York City; Opinion Access, a market research organization; and a food delivery service for supermarkets.

Philadelphia

The Rational Emotive Spiritual Therapy (REST) Inmate Restoration and Aftercare Program helps offenders overcome criminal behavior through combined cognitive therapy (viewed as a promising approach to changing behavior) and spiritual intervention. The REST program began in 2000 in prisons across the five institutions of the Philadelphia Prison System. There is now a reentry aftercare component with a small number of participants.

The program operates differently in each of the prisons, but the core program remains the same. It consists of 13 weeks of group sessions, running approximately 90 minutes each week. The sessions are led by a trained, certified volunteer counselor. Once inmates complete their course work, they graduate and are paired with a mentor before they are released. The mentor helps them connect to community-based faith groups that can direct them to resources for training and employment assistance. The aftercare part of the program is not mandatory.

The program relies heavily on volunteers, who go through extensive training and must pass an exam to

become a certified group counselor. About 1,000 inmates participate in the program each year, and since the program's inception, more than 1,400 inmates have graduated.[7] In one survey of REST participants, 84 percent of the inmates said the program had been very useful to them.[8]

The Promise of Faith-Based Programs

As these five programs illustrate, faith-based programs — both prison-based and community-based — can provide much needed services. Government agencies, given their structure and specific missions, can find it difficult to match some of these services. For example, faith-based groups provide assistance that draws upon and reflects community values and culture.[9] Their position within the community offers ties that are perhaps most important for giving offenders a better chance for success when they return home.

Corrections-related faith-based programs offer the potential to reduce the cost of service provision through the contributions of committed volunteers. This may help explain the proliferation of faith-based programs throughout the United States.[10] Given this, further evaluations of the effectiveness of such programs could garner information useful to correctional institutions nationwide. Several of the programs discussed earlier are working toward this goal by incorporating evidence-based practices into their curricula and developing program structures that support evaluation.

ENDNOTES

[1] Solomon, Amy L., Michelle Waul, Asheley Van Ness and Jeremy Travis. 2001. *Reentry and the faith community.* Briefing paper. In *Outside the Walls Guide: A National snapshot of community-based prisoner reentry programs,* 162-165. Washington D.C.: Urban Institute. Accessed July 30, 2007 at www. reentrymediaoutreach.org/resourceguide .htm.

[2] The five programs were studied by Caterina Roman and her colleagues at the Urban Institute, Washington, D.C. Their 2006 final report is: *Evaluability studies of faith-based programs in corrections,* final report submitted to the National Institute of

Justice, U.S. Department of Justice. Available at www. ncjrs.gov/pdffiles1/nij/grants/ 209350. pdf.

[3] Horizon Communities in Prison. 2006. State Reports: Ohio, Recidivism data. Winter Park, Fla.: Horizon Communities in Prison. Accessed February 2007 at http:// horizoncommunities.org/Marion.htm.

[4] Hughes, Timothy and Doris James Wilson. 2000. *Reentry trends in the United States: Inmates returning to the community after serving time in prison.* Washington, D.C.: Bureau of Justice Statistics, U.S. Department of Justice. Available at www. ojp.usdoj.gov/bjs/reentry/reentry.htm.

[5] Florida Department of Corrections. Update on faith- and character-based institutions. Accessed February 2007 at www. dc.state.fl.us/oth/faith/stats.html.

[6] O'Connor, Thomas, Tim Cayton, Scott Taylor, Rick McKenna and Norm Monroe. 2004. Home for Good in Oregon: A community, faith and state re-entry partnership to increase restorative justice. *Corrections Today,* 66(6):72-76. Alexandria, Va.: American Correctional Association.

[7] I-REST Inc. Web site. Accessed February 2007 at www.restphilly.com/training center.html and www.restphilly.com/rest phillyproject.html.

[8] Cnann, Ram A. and Jill Sinha, 2004. *Back into the fold: Helping ex-prisoners reconnect through faith.* Baltimore: Annie E. Casey Foundation. (January). Available at www.aecf.org/upload/PublicationFiles/FF36 22H352.pdf.

Roman, J., M. Kane, E. Turner and B. Frazier. 2006. *Instituting lasting reforms for prisoner reentry in Philadelphia.* Washington, D.C.: Urban Institute, Justice Policy Center. (June). Available at www.urban. org/UploadedPDF/411345_lastingreforms. pdf.

[9] Hercik, J., R. Lewis and B. Myles. 2004. *Development of a guide to resources on faith-based organizations in criminal justice,* final report to the National Institute of Justice. Fairfax, Va.: Caliber Associates. Available at www.ncjrs.gov/pdf files1/nij/grants/ 209350. pdf.

[10] Solomon et al. 2001.

Laurie C. Bright is a senior social science analyst for the National Institute of Justice, Office of Justice Programs, U.S. Department of Justice. Mary G. Graham, a freelance writer and former director of communications at NIJ, helped in developing the article.

New Report On Juvenile Detention Reform Released

A new report shows that reducing the use of pretrial juvenile detention resulted in systemwide juvenile justice improvements.

The report, *Beyond Detention: System Transformation through Juvenile Detention Reform,* documents the reforms inspired by the Juvenile Detention Alternatives Initiative (JDAI), a nationally-renowned, data-driven and outcome-based collaborative effort aimed at ensuring that detention is used only when appropriate.

In three model sites that have followed key detention reform strategies, communities reduced racial disparities, sent fewer youths to state youth prisons,increased the involvement of families and youths in their rehabilitation, and improved the juvenile justice systems' ability to make appropriate decisions about where youths should be supervised to protect public safety and receive services. *Beyond Detention: System Transformation through Juvenile Detention Reform* is the 14th monograph in the series "Pathway's to Juvenile Detention Reform," published by the Annie E. Casey Foundation, and is available on the JDAI Help Desk Web site at www.jdaihelpdesk.org.

Correlating Incarcerated Mothers, Foster Care and Mother-Child Reunification

By Marilyn C. Moses

Author's note: *Points of view expressed in this article do not represent the official position or policies of the U.S. Department of Justice.*

Is a mother's incarceration directly responsible for her child's placement in foster care, and how likely is a mother to be reunited with her child? Interim findings from an ongoing NIJ-funded study[1] revealed surprising answers: most incarcerated mothers lost their children to foster care prior to incarceration and most are very unlikely to be reunited with their children.

The study, which was jointly funded by the National Institute of Justice (NIJ), the Open Society Institute, The Chicago Community Trust and the Russell Sage Foundation, was awarded to researchers at the Universities of California and Chicago. The researchers focused on mothers who were incarcerated in Illinois State prisons and the Cook County Jail in Chicago from 1990 to 2000[2] to examine the relationship between a mother's imprisonment and the probability that her child would be placed in foster care. They also studied the children's foster care placement outcomes (see Figure 1).

Which Came First?

Researchers found that 27 percent of the incarcerated mothers had a child who had been placed in foster care at some point during the child's life. Surprisingly, researchers found that in most cases the mother's incarceration was not the reason the child was placed in foster care. In almost three-quarters of the cases, the child was placed in foster care prior to his or her mother's first incarceration. And in more than 40 percent of those cases, the child entered foster care as many as three years before his or her mother went to jail.

This finding contradicts a widely held assumption that children are placed in foster care as a direct result of their mothers' incarceration. The early findings indicate that a child's foster care status is rarely a direct result of a mother's imprisonment.

Likelihood of Mother-Child Reunification

Researchers also compared the outcomes for the children of these incarcerated mothers with outcomes for all children in foster care. Figure 1 shows that other children in foster care are twice as likely to reunite with their parents as children of incarcerated mothers in foster care. Additionally, children of imprisoned mothers are more likely to be adopted than all children in foster care. This could be for a number of reasons, but mostly because many of the children are placed in kinship/foster care, where they are taken care of by other relatives who adopt them.

Perhaps most notable is that children of incarcerated mothers were four times more likely to be "still in" foster care than all other children (see Figure 1). These children linger in foster care until they are 18 when they "age out" of the system; they do not reunify with their parents, get adopted, enter into subsidized guardianship, go into independent living or leave through some other means. Moreover, another recent study has found that children who "age out" have a high probability of ending up incarcerated as adults, regardless of whether their parents were incarcerated or not.[3]

Getting The Research Right

The interim findings from the study represent a significant step forward in the development of knowledge regarding incarcerated parents and their children. Until now, no study of this magnitude focused exclusively on the status of children of incarcerated parents. Instead, researchers had focused primarily on the incarcerated parent; data on children and their custody status were incidental to that inquiry.

Previously, several other factors also impeded research on these children: small sample sizes; reluctance of incarcerated parents, family members, and caregivers to provide information that might disrupt formal or informal custody arrangements; reliance on self-report; and insufficient funding and resources to locate and track children over time.

NIJ Builds on Prior Research

The interim findings from this study are the latest in NIJ's 15-year history of work in this area. In 1992 the field asked NIJ to provide a practical research-to-practice solution to address the needs of these at-risk

> Until now, no study of this magnitude focused exclusively on the status of children of incarcerated parents.

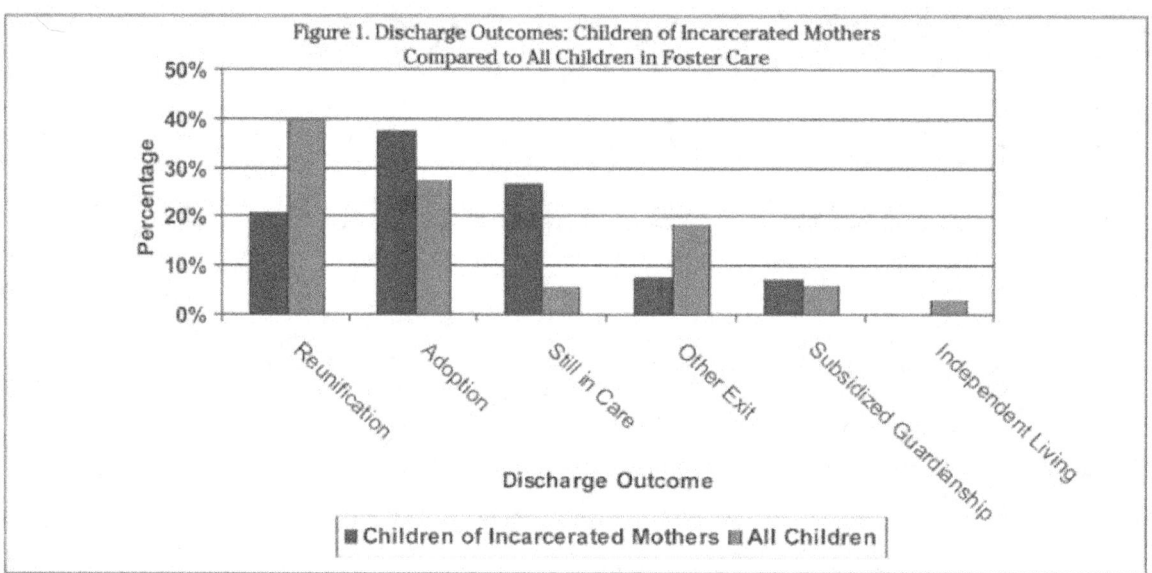

Figure 1. Discharge Outcomes: Children of Incarcerated Mothers Compared to All Children in Foster Care

children, their imprisoned parents, and the lack of visitation between parent and child. NIJ responded by creating a first-of-its-kind partnership between an adult correctional institution and a major youth service organization — the Girl Scouts Beyond Bars[4] program — and tested its feasibility. This program has since been replicated in more than 20 states and 40 correctional institutions across the country and has won several national awards. Recently, the Public Broadcasting System (PBS or public television) aired a nationally televised documentary on this program, and it was also recently replicated by a boys' youth service organization.[5]

Since the early 1990s, NIJ has conducted research on female offenders, reentry and family reunification efforts. One publication resulting from this effort was the NIJ Program Focus, *Women's Prison Association: Supporting Women Offenders and Their Families.*[6] This effort was followed in the late 1990s by two studies on incarcerated fathers and their children. The first examined the attitudes and perceptions of incarcerated men toward child care and raising children.[7] The second study was a three-year ethnographic examination of the effects of male incarceration on families in the District of Columbia.[8]

While significant, NIJ's research efforts were generally frustrated by the same barriers that had stymied others — small sample sizes, reliance on self-report, and the lack of funding and resources for a long-range study

of such children. The researchers at the universities of California and Chicago have the potential to push the field forward in building knowledge in this evolving discipline. The study's reliance on large administrative datasets provides objective and verifiable data on very large samples of incarcerated mothers and their children over a decade. It offers the opportunity to shed light on a population about which we have had many speculations, but, until now, very little reliable data.

... while there are more children affected by a father's incarceration due to the overwhelming majority of men in prison, a child's stability appears to be most threatened by a mother's incarceration.

What Is Next?

Researchers from the universities of Chicago and California will continue to examine other questions posed by the relationship between child welfare and parental incarceration, such as:

- Do families in which the mother is incarcerated before the child is placed in foster care differ from families in which the child is removed before the parent is incarcerated?
- What effect does the mother's incarceration have on termination of parental rights?
- What is the relationship between the offense that resulted in the mother's incarceration and the types of child maltreatment that prompted child welfare services to intervene?
- What are the similarities and differences between the mother's type of incarceration (jail or prison) and the child welfare issues?

The researchers hope that answers to these questions will illuminate the crossroads of the foster care and criminal justice systems and provide information that will have important implications for both practitioners and policy-makers. As well noted in the field, while there are more children affected by a father's incarceration due to the overwhelming majority of men in

prison, a child's stability appears to be most threatened by a mother's incarceration.[9] Thus, future findings could guide efforts to develop crime prevention and family reunification strategies — especially for mother and child — and create other effective collaborative efforts between the corrections and child welfare systems.

ENDNOTES

[1] National Institute of Justice. Ongoing Study, Intersections of Prisons and Child Welfare: Findings From One State Using Administrative Data. October 2006-December 2006.

[2] Researchers looked at 52,883 incarcerated or formerly incarcerated mothers and 124,626 of their children to determine that 7,281 incarcerated or formerly incarcerated mothers had 21,533 children that, at some point in time, went into foster care.

[3] Courtney, M.E., S. Terao, and N.Bost. 2004. Midwest evaluations of the adult functioning of former youth: Conditions of youth preparing to leave state care in Illinois. Chicago. Chapin Hall Center for Children, University of Chicago.

[4] Originally known as Girl Scouts Behind Bars. See Moses, Marilyn. 1995. Keeping incarcerated mothers and their daughters together: Girl Scouts beyond bars. Washington, D.C.: U.S. Department of Justice, National Institute of Justice. Available at www.ncjrs.gov/pdffiles/girlsct.pdf. See also: Moses, Marilyn C. 1995. Synergistic solution for children of incarcerated parents: Girl Scouts beyond bars. *Corrections Today*, 57(7):124-126.

[5] Stripling, Sherry. 2005. New Boy Scout program takes boys behind bars — to see mom. The Seattle Times, p.1.1. (May 8).

[6] Conly, Catherine. 1998. Women's prison association: Supporting women offenders and their families. Washington, D.C.: U.S. Department of Justice, National Institute of Justice. Available at www.ojp.usdoj.gov/nij/pubs-sum/172858.htm.

[7] Mendez, Garry. 2001. Incarcerated men and their children: Study report. Final report available at www.ncjrs.gov/pdffiles1/nij/grants/189789.pdf.

[8] Braman, Donald. 2003. Families and incarceration. Final report available at www.ncjrs.gov/pdffiles1/nij/grants/202981.pdf. This report was later published as a book: Braman, Donald. 2004. Doing Time on the Outside. Ann Arbor: University of Michigan Press.

[9] Mumula, Christopher J. 2000. Incarcerated parents and their children. Washington, D.C.: U.S. Department of Justice, Bureau of Justice Statistics.

Marilyn C. Moses is a social science analyst in NIJ's Office of Research and Evaluation. For more information, contact her at (202) 514-6205 or marilyn.moses@usdoj.gov.

Factories Behind Fences: Do Prison 'Real Work' Programs Work?

By Marilyn C. Moses and Cindy J. Smith, Ph.D.

About the Authors

Ms. Moses is a social science analyst at the National Institute of Justice. Dr. Smith is the chief of NIJ's International Center.

When someone is in prison, does having a real job with real pay yield benefits when he or she is released? Findings from an evaluation funded by the National Institute of Justice (NIJ) suggest that this might be the case.

Offenders who worked for private companies while imprisoned obtained employment more quickly, maintained employment longer, and had lower recidivism rates than those who worked in traditional correctional industries or were involved in "other-than-work" (OTW) activities.

"Factories behind fences" is not a new idea. Traditional industries (TI)—in which offenders are supervised by corrections staff and work for a modest sum—have been a mainstay of corrections for more than 150 years. Examples of traditional industries include the manufacture of signs, furniture,

and garments, as well as the stereotypical license plates. By obtaining work experience in these industries, inmates acquire the skills they need to secure gainful employment upon release and avoid recidivism.

Another program—the Prison Industry Enhancement Certification Program (PIECP)—allows inmates to work for a private employer in a "free world" occupation and earn the prevailing wage. Created by Congress in 1979, PIECP encourages State and local correctional agencies to form partnerships with private companies to give inmates real work opportunities.[1] Over the years, PIECP operations have included the manufacture of aluminum screens and windows for Solar Industries, Inc.; circuit boards for Joint Venture Electronics; street sweeper brushes for United Rotary Brush Corporation; corrugated boxes for PRIDE Box; gloves for Hawkeye Glove Manufacturing, Inc.; and the manufacture and refurbishment of Shelby Cobra automobiles for Shelby American Management Co. Other PIECP operations include alfalfa

production for Five Dot Land and Cattle Company; papaya packing for Tropical Hawaiian Products; potato processing for Floyd Wilcox & Sons; and boat-building for Misty Harbor.

PIECP seeks to:

- Generate products and services that enable prisoners to make a contribution to society, offset the cost of incarceration, support family members, and compensate crime victims.

- Reduce prison idleness, increase inmate job skills, and improve the prospects for prisoners' successful transition to the community upon release.

More than 70,000 inmates—an average of 2,500 per year—have participated in PIECP since the program's inception. By the end of 2005, 6,555 offenders were employed in the program. Although this number reflects a 285 percent increase in PIECP positions in the past decade, it represents only a small fraction of the total number of inmates in our Nation's State prisons and local jails.

Does the Program Work?

In a sense, PIECP can be thought of as a grand experiment. After 28 years, the obvious question is: Does it work?

To find out, NIJ teamed with the U.S. Department of Justice's Bureau of Justice Assistance to fund the first national evaluation of PIECP. Researchers at the University of Baltimore compared a group of post-release inmates who worked in PIECP with inmates from two other groups—those who worked in TI and those involved in OTW activities, including idleness.[2] Cindy J. Smith, Ph.D., one of the authors of this article, was part of that research team. Then at the University of Baltimore, Smith and her colleagues considered two questions:

- Does PIECP participation increase post-release employment more than work in TI and OTW programs?

- Does PIECP participation reduce recidivism more than work in TI or OTW programs?

A WORD OF CAUTION: SELECTION BIAS

Although the results of the Prison Industry Enhancement Certification Program (PIECP) study are positive—showing better outcomes for participants in the PIECP group compared to the traditional industries (TI) and the other-than-work (OTW) groups—they do not definitively show that the better outcomes were due to PIECP itself. This is because the participants in the three groups were not randomly assigned to the groups, a process that ensures that the differences in results are due to the program, rather than to preexisting differences among the participants.

How then were participants in this study assigned to the different groups? First, prisoners volunteered to participate in a work program. They were then interviewed by prospective employers in both the TI program and PIECP. Therefore, inmates who worked in either the TI program or PIECP were "self-selected" and may have had different motivations and backgrounds than the OTW inmates, the third group studied, which may have led to better outcomes. This concern, known as selection bias, can be definitively ruled out only by random assignment to groups that are going to be compared. In this study, selection bias seems a larger concern when comparing the volunteers (that is, PIECP and TI participants) to the non-volunteers (the OTW group) than in comparing the results of the two employment (PIECP and TI) groups.

The researchers in this study attempted to ensure that the groups were comparable by matching inmates in the three groups using a number of factors, including demographics and time served. Nevertheless, this matching may not have completely eliminated the selection bias. Therefore, the results should be interpreted with caution.

Although the findings are not conclusive, they are positive. (See sidebar, "A Word of Caution: Selection Bias.") Researchers found that, after they were released, PIECP participants found jobs more quickly and held them longer than did their counterparts in the TI and OTW groups. Approximately 55 percent of PIECP workers obtained employment within the first quarter after release. Only 40 percent of their counterparts found employment within that time.

Nearly 49 percent of PIECP participants were employed continuously for more than 1 year, whereas 40.4 percent of the offenders in TI and 38.5 percent of the offenders in OTW programs were continuously employed for that length of time.

Length of Continuous Employment Postrelease			
Length of Employment	Percent of PIECP Group	Percent of Traditional Industries Group	Percent of Other-Than-Work Group
1 year+	48.6	40.4	38.5
3 years+	13.7	10.3	10.3

Three years out, PIECP participants performed better than releasees from the TI or OTW groups. Almost 14 percent of PIECP releasees were employed for 3 continuous years, but only 10.3 percent of the other offenders maintained constant employment for that same period of time. (See chart above, "Length of Continuous Employment Postrelease.")

Examining wages earned by the participants after they were released, the researchers found that the PIECP group earned more than the TI and OTW groups. Of all the releasees, however, 55 percent did not earn wages equal to a full-time job at the Federal minimum wage. Because the data available to the researchers reported total earnings only and not the number of hours worked, it was impossible to determine whether this was because the releasees were: (1) working part-time, (2) working intermittently, or (3) earning less than the Federal minimum wage.

Recidivism

The researchers measured recidivism rates for all three groups using the traditional yardsticks: new arrest, conviction, and incarceration.[3] The results showed that PIECP releasees had lower rates of rearrest, conviction, and incarceration than offenders who were in the TI or the OTW groups.

At the end of the first year postrelease, 82 percent of PIECP participants were arrest free. The average amount of time from release to first arrest for PIECP participants was approximately 993 days (slightly less than 3 years). At 1 year postrelease, offenders in the TI and OTW groups remained arrest free at approximately the same rate (77 percent and 76 percent, respectively) as PIECP participants. By

3 years out, however, the arrest-free rates for all three groups declined to 60 percent for the PIECP participants and 52 percent for offenders in the TI and OTW programs.

Looking at conviction and reincarceration rates, the researchers found that 77 percent of PIECP participants were conviction free during the followup periods, compared to 73 percent of the OTW group. Ninety-three percent of PIECP participants remained incarceration free during the followup periods, compared to 89 percent of the OTW participants.

Inmate PIECP Wages

Wages earned by PIECP participants in prison benefit taxpayers in addition to helping the inmates themselves. Although the program requires a percentage of PIECP wages to be saved to assist the inmate when he is released, the remaining wages make their way back into the national economy, either directly or indirectly. A significant portion of the wages earned by prisoners in the program, for example, goes directly to the State to cover the cost of prisoner room and board. PIECP wages also provide child support and alimony to family members, as well as restitution to crime victims. (See chart on p. 35, "Distribution of PIECP Wages.")

An Underutilized Rehabilitation Option?

The research suggests that PIECP has been successful. Inmate PIECP wages benefit inmates, taxpayers, victims, families, and States. PIECP participants also acquire postrelease jobs more quickly, retain these jobs longer, and return to the criminal justice system less frequently and at a lower rate than inmates who worked in traditional

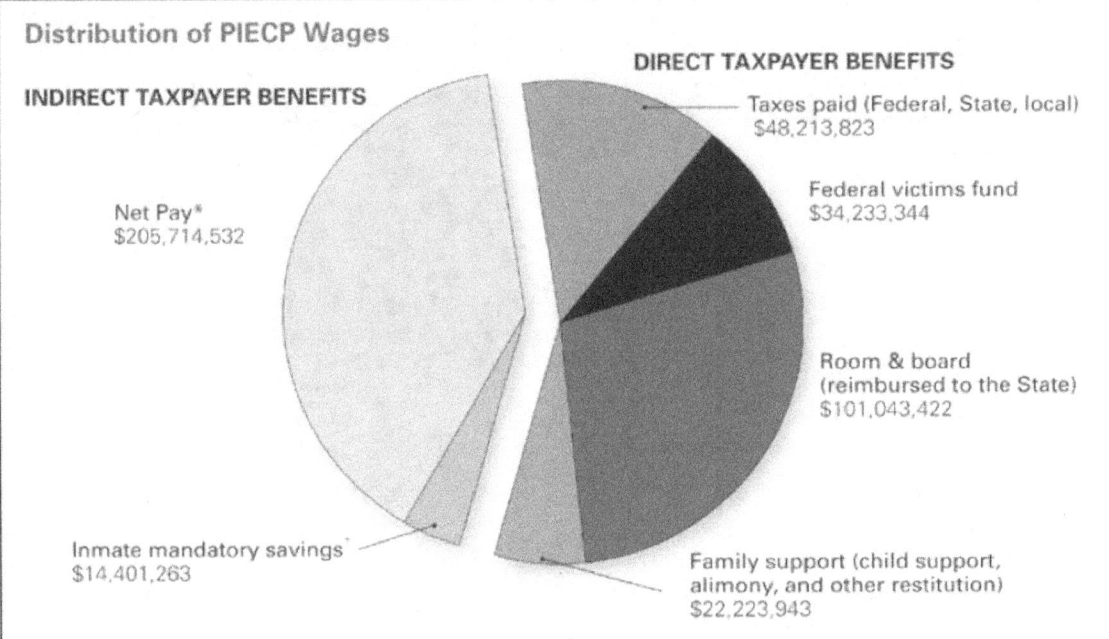

Distribution of PIECP Wages

INDIRECT TAXPAYER BENEFITS

Net Pay*
$205,714,532

Inmate mandatory savings†
$14,401,263

DIRECT TAXPAYER BENEFITS

Taxes paid (Federal, State, local)
$48,213,823

Federal victims fund
$34,233,344

Room & board
(reimbursed to the State)
$101,043,422

Family support (child support,
alimony, and other restitution)
$22,223,943

Source: Data compiled (under OJP/BJA grant number 2006-DD-BX-K010) by Sahra Nadiir, program coordinator of the National Correctional Industries Association's PIECP, based on information submitted to the Bureau of Justice Assistance by PIECP certificate holders.

*An inmate's net pay covers his living expenses, such as food and toiletries, and some health care costs, such as co-pays and prescription drugs. Typically, the money to pay for such expenses would come from taxpayers.

† Under PIECP, 10 percent of a PIECP participant's wages is set aside for the inmate's use upon release.

industries or engaged in other-than-work activities. These findings suggest that PIECP is an underutilized rehabilitation option and that additional efforts to increase the number of PIECP jobs could have an important impact on the Nation's prison and jail populations.

NCJ 218264

For More Information

- Smith, C.J., J. Bechtel, A. Patrick, R.R. Smith, and L. Wilson-Gentry, *Correctional Industries Preparing Inmates for Re-entry: Recidivism and Post-release Employment,* final report submitted to the National Institute of Justice, Washington, DC: June 2006 (NCJ 214608), available at www.ncjrs.gov/pdffiles1/nij/grants/214608.pdf.

- Petersik, T., T. Nayak, and M.K. Foreman, *Identifying Beneficiaries of PIE Inmate Incomes,* The National Correctional

Industries Association, July 31, 2003, available at www.nationalcia.org/researchfullrpt.pdf.

Notes

1. With the exception of PIECP, U.S. jail and prison inmates are prohibited, under the Amhurst-Sumners Act of 1935, from producing goods for sale in open interstate commercial markets; PIECP-certified programs are exempt from the $10,000 limit on the sale of prisoner-made goods to the Federal Government.

2. The sample size included 6,464 inmates, with subjects nearly equally divided among groups. The sample included offenders released from 46 prisons in 5 States that implemented PIECP from January 1, 1996, to June 30, 2001. The followup period began on the day the inmate was released and ranged from slightly under 2 years to 7.5 years.

3. Technical violations were not considered new arrests.

Habilitation or Harm: Project Greenlight and the Potential Consequences of Correctional Programming
by James A. Wilson, Ph.D.

About the Author
Dr. Wilson is an assistant professor of sociology at Fordham University in New York.

Not long ago, I facilitated a discussion among policymakers, criminal justice professionals, and representatives from community organizations about the large number of incarcerated individuals, the recidivism rate after release, and the effect of both on resources, especially local jails.

As we discussed what we know about effective rehabilitative programming, one attendee could not contain his ire. He strongly asserted that the individuals in his jails had been in program after program after program until they had been programmed nearly to death, and it had not made a whit of difference.

I believe he took offense when I asked him what evidence he had that they actually were good programs and that they worked.

"We know they're good programs—and they don't work," he responded.

His response is emblematic of the continuing nationwide debate on rehabilitation and correctional programs. The perceived failure of prison to deter criminal behavior—as evidenced by high recidivism rates and the substantial costs associated with an increasing number of ex-prisoners who unsuccessfully return to the community— has renewed interest in promising rehabilitative approaches. Nothing has fueled this renewed interest like the recent discussions on Project Greenlight.

Project Greenlight was a short-term, prison-based reentry demonstration program. It was jointly operated by the New York State Department of Correctional Services and the New York State Division of Parole and administered by program developers from the Vera Institute of Justice. Here, I offer a basic overview of the program and, most

importantly, discuss the somewhat contro-versial findings from an evaluation sponsored by the National Institute of Justice.[1]

What Did Project Greenlight Offer?

Offenders tend to leave prison much as they enter: lacking practical and interpersonal skills and possessing few economic and social resources. They tend to encounter significant barriers, both formal and informal, when they return to the community.[2] In an effort to help offenders meet some of these challenges, Project Greenlight was designed as an intensive, prison-based reentry pro-gram to be delivered during the 8 weeks immediately preceding an inmate's release from prison.

The developers of the Project Greenlight program drew extensively from the litera-ture on correctional interventions and from anecdotal evidence about the services that offenders need to succeed when they return home. The key elements of Project Greenlight were:

- **Cognitive-behavioral skills training.** The foundation of the Project Greenlight program was cognitive-behavioral skills training because the research indicates that this type of program shows the most consistent results in reducing offender recidivism.[3] Cognitive-behavioral pro-gramming is based on the theory that if offenders commit crime due to poor socialization, they can be resocialized toward more prosocial thinking and behavior.

- **Employment.** Project Greenlight employed a job counselor to work with program participants on how to write a résumé and improve their interview skills. If inmates were perceived to be job-ready, the counselor matched them with employment opportunities that might lead to stable work upon release.

- **Housing.** Because homeless shelters generally do not provide good living situations, the program worked with the New York City Department of Homeless Services to find short- and long-term housing for inmates who did not have a place to go upon release.

- **Drug education and awareness.** Participants were required to attend drug education or relapse prevention classes to help them deal with addictive behaviors.

- **Family counseling.** When a person returns home after a long absence, the adjustment can be difficult for the entire family. A counselor worked in the evenings with some Project Greenlight participants and their families to help them prepare for the inevitable strains that arise when an absent family member returns home.

- **Practical skills training.** Classes in practical skills offered guidance to Project Greenlight participants on a wide variety of tasks—some straightforward, such as how to use a subway card; some complex, such as how to open and manage a bank account, access emer-gency sources of food or cash, and regain voting rights. The program also helped participants obtain proper identification documents and Medicaid coverage before leaving prison.

- **Community-based networks.** Project Greenlight developed a network of community-based organizations to provide participants with social support after they were released.

- **Familiarity with parole.** Participants were introduced to parole officers and familiarized with the parole process to promote greater adherence to the conditions of parole.

- **Individualized release plan.** Project Greenlight staff worked one-on-one with participants to develop an individualized release plan. At its most basic level, this plan was akin to a "day planner," remind-ing offenders what they planned to do upon release and when they would do it. The plan also attempted to provide a degree of structure to the participants' postrelease activities, helping them add order to what was likely to be a very disorienting time. The release plan was given to the participants' parole officers to make them aware of the goals and tasks established by parolees before their release.

The Greenlight Study

In the Project Greenlight Study, 735 inmates were divided into three groups and followed for at least 1 year (some for 2 years) after release. The intervention group of 334 inmates received the Project Greenlight programming. One comparison group (referred to as the UPS group) comprised 113 inmates who were released directly from prisons in upstate New York without any pre-release services. The second comparison group comprised 278 inmates who participated in the transitional services program (TSP) already in existence at the facility (in the same prison as the Greenlight participants).

Project Greenlight was designed to emphasize specific services that would improve certain interim quality-of-life outcomes and, as a result, would affect subsequent criminal behavior. The developers believed, for example, that helping parolees (who would otherwise end up in a homeless shelter) find stable housing would reduce criminal behavior. The program also had a job counselor to help participants develop their interview skills and connect with potential employers, with the goal of better employment, gained more quickly, for a longer duration.

Interim Quality-of-Life Outcomes

Data from evaluation surveys of participants and parole officers indicated:

- **Employment, family relationships, and use of homeless shelter.** There were no differences between the Project Greenlight group and the control groups.

- **Parole knowledge and adherence.** Although Project Greenlight participants demonstrated significantly more familiarity with parole conditions and were more positive about parole, there was no difference in adherence to parole conditions between the Project Greenlight group and the control groups.

- **Service referrals and contacts.** Project Greenlight participants received more service referrals and reported more contacts with community services after release.

Recidivism Outcomes

Project Greenlight participants showed worse outcomes for every type of recidivism at 6 and 12 months after release. The chart on p. 5, "Percent of Participants Who Recidivated at 6 and 12 Months," shows the percentage of each group that experienced any kind of arrest (misdemeanor or felony), felony arrest only, and parole revocation. It is especially noteworthy—because it is statistically significant—that the overall arrest rate for the Project Greenlight group was 10 percent higher than that for the TSP group at 12 months post-release (34 percent versus 24 percent). Also statistically significant is the 12 percent more parole revocations experienced by the Project Greenlight group than the UPS group at 12 months post-release (25 percent versus 13 percent).

Several findings of the evaluation were at odds with program expectations. Most notably, Project Greenlight participants' postrelease outcomes were significantly worse than those of the TSP and UPS groups. The evaluation found that the Project Greenlight program had no effect on the interim outcomes that it was designed to address—including housing, employment, and parole—and that Project Greenlight participants fared significantly worse than the two control groups in rearrest and parole revocation rates at the 1-year mark. In addition, although Project Greenlight participants displayed greater knowledge of parole conditions, showed more positive attitudes toward parole, received more service referrals, and reported greater contact with service providers after release, none of these translated into better outcomes.

Why Did Project Greenlight Participants Do Worse?

Project Greenlight had been viewed positively by many people: program developers and staff, participants, corrections officials, policymakers, and community advocates. Why, therefore, were the results so different from the perceptions? Why did the Project Greenlight intervention fail to reduce recidivism? Indeed, why did

Percent of Participants Who Recidivated at 6 and 12 Months

Recidivism Outcome	Project Greenlight (344 inmates)	TSP (278 inmates)	UPS (113 inmates)
All arrests			
6 months	17.2	13.0	14.4
12 months	34.1*	24.2*	26.8
Felony arrests			
6 months	8.3	6.6	7.2
12 months	18.0	13.0	12.0
Parole revocations			
6 months	9.8	9.4	7.4
12 months	25.1*	21.0	13.2*

* Difference in the indicated pairs (by row) is statistically significant at $p < .05$.

participants show substantially worse outcomes than both of the control groups?

Although selection bias is always a potential concern—did more crime-prone individuals end up in the Project Greenlight group than in the control groups?—the strength of the evaluation (both design and methodology) suggests that selection bias was not responsible for the negative outcomes. A more likely explanation is that something associated with the program or its implementation contributed to the negative findings. There are several potential explanations.[4]

Obviously, Project Greenlight's curricula had the potential to yield positive outcomes. It also had the potential to result in no difference among the three groups, but it is difficult to imagine that the program's practical-skills or cognitive-behavioral training, for example, were somehow inherently criminogenic. The same curricula have been used extensively elsewhere, under a variety of conditions with a diversity of populations, with positive outcomes. It is therefore highly unlikely that the program's content was responsible for the negative results.

It seems equally unlikely that referrals to community organizations, housing providers, and other community services would lead the Project Greenlight group to be rearrested at higher rates. In short, the program curricula seem relatively innocuous in their potential for creating negative outcomes.

There are reasons to suspect, however, that program implementation, including program design, might have resulted in the negative outcomes.

First, the standard cognitive-behavioral program that, in the past, has produced robust results in reducing offender recidivism was radically restructured in the Project Greenlight program. The recommended class size for cognitive-skills training is 10 to 13 participants; the Project Greenlight class size was 26. Given that many incarcerated people have limited interpersonal skills and education and are likely to be impulsive, a small class size is considered crucial in helping them maintain attention and helping instructors deliver material.

The cognitive-behavior model upon which Project Greenlight was based typically delivers services twice weekly for 4–6 months. The Project Greenlight program compressed the delivery of services, however, into daily classes for 8 weeks. These and other changes to the standard cognitive-behavior program model raise questions about how effective Project Greenlight could have been considering the deviations from what has long been considered the optimal program. In addition, participants in the Project Greenlight group were transferred from one prison to another—and were required to participate—suggesting the possibility that they could have been overwhelmed and perhaps even frustrated and angry about their participation.

The relatively short nature of the program might not have given participants enough time to get past any negative emotions and resistance generated by coerced participation.

Although the developers of Project Greenlight drew elements from the literature on correctional interventions, there were some key failures—most notably, ignoring the treatment principles that form the foundation of effective programming. There is general agreement that interventions should be directed toward high-risk participants and that assessing risk and needs should be a part of any intervention protocol. Project Greenlight staff found, however, that the assessment tool was too cumbersome and time-consuming to administer and therefore dropped it.

Another basic treatment principle is that interventions should target participants' specific needs. Project Greenlight was a broad-based intervention in which everyone in the group was exposed to the same program elements. Postrelease interviews indicated that some participants felt significant frustration and anger about being forced to attend drug education sessions when they had no history of substance use. It should also be noted that an emerging body of evidence suggests that the delivery of intensive services to low-risk individuals may be counterproductive.[5]

In addition to program design problems, Project Greenlight could have been poorly implemented. As a general proposition, implementation has clearly been identified as one of the most significant obstacles to an effective intervention.[6] The evaluation found a correlation between Project Greenlight participants who worked with specific case managers and the program's negative outcomes. Additionally, some participants in the Greenlight group were observed to be disengaged and appeared uninterested.

Project Greenlight attempted to create a comprehensive intervention by pulling together diverse program elements to address the multiple needs of participants. The program was clearly attractive to policymakers and corrections officials because of its short duration and the large number of individuals who could receive the programming. Based on the evaluation, however, one can seriously question whether Project Greenlight was a "hodgepodge of unproven and unstandardized clinical interventions" all lumped together.[7] Although this may seem to be a harsh characterization, it might be an accurate portrayal of the program that was finally implemented.

What Have We Learned?

I considered beginning this article, as many discussions of corrections do, with the standard description of the U.S. social experiment in mass incarceration: the consequences to our society, communities, and families of having more than 2 million people incarcerated and nearly 700,000 admitted to and released from prison every year. I hope, however, that the experience I described in the opening of this article demonstrates the frustration of many criminal justice professionals. We do not really know about many of the programs currently being used, and some real lessons can be learned from the negative outcomes of a program like Project Greenlight.

First, whenever an intervention is contemplated and implemented, there is always an implicit assumption that "good" is going to come of it. Human behavior is complex, however, and we are still trying to understand it in a variety of ways, from the biological to the sociological to the philosophical. Perhaps we should also hold the assumption that an intervention program might do harm. Clearly, the implementation of every program should have precisely stated outcomes and a way to assess those outcomes on a regular basis.

Second, the "what works" literature on correctional interventions discusses programming that is known to work. Often, these discussions focus on the programs themselves without exploring why they work. The treatment principles that underlie effective programming were often ignored in Project Greenlight. This opened the program developers to the critique that they created a "kitchen sink" program[8]—and one with negative outcomes at that.

Third, although Project Greenlight was labeled a reentry demonstration program, it had in fact no real reentry component. It was prison-based, with no structured followup in the community. Given what the reentry literature says about the need for postrelease services, it appears that an individualized release plan such as the one developed for Project Greenlight participants does not provide the necessary structured followup. Some States recognize the potential for structured postrelease assistance—for example, although still untested, Connecticut's Building Bridges program allows parolees to work with a case manager for up to 1 year after release.[3]

Finally, it is crucial to recognize that if Project Greenlight had not been evaluated, the program would be regarded as an unqualified success, based solely on the positive perceptions of those involved. Despite all the promise and positive perceptions, the program resulted in more harm than good. Could there be a clearer example of why program evaluations are needed?

I can understand the frustration expressed by the professional I mentioned in the opening of this article. We might continue to talk about the positives of rehabilitation, but when practitioners and the public see the constant churning of individuals through the criminal justice system, they see a failed system based on programs that do not work. If we continue to place offenders in programs that are positively perceived but that remain untested, we might continue to produce outcomes similar to Project Greenlight. Without effective evaluations of our programs, we run the risk of programming offenders nearly to death—and it still will not make one whit of difference.

NCJ 218258

For More Information

■ Wilson, J.A., and R. Davis, "Hard Realities Meet Good Intentions: An Evaluation of the Project Greenlight Reentry Program," *Criminology and Public Policy* 5 (2) (2006): 303–338.

■ Brown, B., R. Campbell, J.A. Wilson, Y. Cheryachukin, R.C. Davis, J. Dauphinee,

R. Hope, K. Gehi, *Smoothing the Path From Prison to Home*, final report submitted to the National Institute of Justice, Washington, DC: 2006 (NCJ 213714), available at www.ncjrs.gov/pdffiles1/nij/grants/213714.pdf.

Notes

1. The JEHT Foundation contributed the initial funding to begin the Project Greenlight evaluation. For more information on the JEHT Foundation, visit www.jehtfoundation.org.

2. This literature has grown extensively. See Travis, J., A. Solomon, and M. Waul, *From Prison to Home: The Dimensions and Consequences of Prisoner Reentry*, Washington, DC: Urban Institute, 2001, available at www.urban.org/UploadedPDF/from_prison_to_home.pdf.

3. More information on cognitive-behavior research is included in Andrews, D.A., I. Zinger, R.D. Hoge, J. Bonta, P. Gendreau, and F.T. Cullen, "Does Correctional Treatment Work? A Clinically Relevant and Psychologically Informed Meta-Analysis," *Criminology* 28 (1990): 369–404.

4. Frank Porporino, codeveloper of the Reasoning and Rehabilitation program—a multifaceted cognitive-behavior program used throughout Canada and the United States to teach juvenile and adult offenders cognitive skills and values—assisted me in clarifying some of my explanations of the negative findings.

5. Lowenkamp, C.T., and E.J. Latessa, "Increasing the Effectiveness of Correctional Programming Through the Risk Principle: Identifying Offenders for Residential Placement," *Criminology and Public Policy* 4 (2) (2005): 263–290.

6. Rhine, E.E., T.L. Mawhorr, and E.C. Parks, "Implementation: The Bane of Effective Correctional Programs," *Criminology and Public Policy* 5 (2) (2006): 347–358.

7. Marlowe, D.B., "When 'What Works' Never Did: Dodging the 'Scarlet M' in Correctional Rehabilitation," *Criminology and Public Policy* 5 (2) (2006): 342.

8. Ibid.

9. For an overview, see the Council of State Governments Web site at www.csgeast.org/pdfs/justicereinvest/BuildingBridges.pdf or www.csgeast.org/pdfs/justicereinvest/BuildingBridgesReportUpdate.pdf.

About the National Institute of Justice

NIJ is the research, development, and evaluation agency of the U.S. Department of Justice. NIJ's mission is to advance scientific research, development, and evaluation to enhance the administration of justice and public safety. NIJ's principal authorities are derived from the Omnibus Crime Control and Safe Streets Act of 1968, as amended (see 42 U.S.C. §§ 3721–3723)

The NIJ Director is appointed by the President and confirmed by the Senate. The Director establishes the Institute's objectives, guided by the priorities of the Office of Justice Programs, the U.S. Department of Justice, and the needs of the field. The Institute actively solicits the views of criminal justice and other professionals and researchers to inform its search for the knowledge and tools to guide policy and practice.

Strategic Goals

NIJ has seven strategic goals grouped into three categories:

Creating relevant knowledge and tools

1. Partner with State and local practitioners and policymakers to identify social science research and technology needs.
2. Create scientific, relevant, and reliable knowledge—with a particular emphasis on terrorism, violent crime, drugs and crime, cost-effectiveness, and community-based efforts—to enhance the administration of justice and public safety.
3. Develop affordable and effective tools and technologies to enhance the administration of justice and public safety.

Dissemination

4. Disseminate relevant knowledge and information to practitioners and policymakers in an understandable, timely, and concise manner.
5. Act as an honest broker to identify the information, tools, and technologies that respond to the needs of stakeholders.

Agency management

6. Practice fairness and openness in the research and development process.
7. Ensure professionalism, excellence, accountability, cost-effectiveness, and integrity in the management and conduct of NIJ activities and programs.

Program Areas

In addressing these strategic challenges, the Institute is involved in the following program areas: crime control and prevention, including policing; drugs and crime; justice systems and offender behavior, including corrections; violence and victimization; communications and information technologies; critical incident response; investigative and forensic sciences, including DNA; less-than-lethal technologies; officer protection; education and training technologies; testing and standards; technology assistance to law enforcement and corrections agencies; field testing of promising programs; and international crime control.

In addition to sponsoring research and development and technology assistance, NIJ evaluates programs, policies, and technologies. NIJ communicates its research and evaluation findings through conferences and print and electronic media.

To find out more about the National Institute of Justice, please visit:

www.ojp.usdoj.gov/nij

or contact:

National Criminal Justice
 Reference Service
P.O. Box 6000
Rockville, MD 20849–6000
800–851–3420
e-mail: askncjrs@ncjrs.org